D0831295

THE NEW TEMPLE SHAKESPEARE

Edited by M. R. Ridley, M.A.

PERICLES

by William Shakespeare

London: J. M. DENT & SONS LTD.
New York: E. P. DUTTON & CO. INC.

All rights reserved
Printed in Great Britain
by Morrison & Gibb Ltd., London and Edinburgh
and decorated by
Eric Gill
for
J. M. Dent & Sons Ltd.
Aldine House, Bedford St. London

| Toronto | . | Vancouver |
| Melbourne | . | Wellington |

First Published in this Edition 1935
Reprinted 1946

Editor's General Note

The Text. The editor has kept before him the aim of presenting to the modern reader the nearest possible approximation to what Shakespeare actually wrote. The text is therefore conservative, and is based on the earliest reliable printed text. But to avoid distraction (*a*) the spelling is modernised, and (*b*) a limited number of universally accepted emendations is admitted without comment. Where a Quarto text exists as well as the First Folio the passages which occur only in the Quarto are enclosed in square brackets [ ] and those which occur only in the Folio in brace brackets { }.

Scene Division. The rapid continuity of the Elizabethan curtainless production is lost by the 'traditional' scene divisions. Where there is an essential difference of place these scene divisions are retained. Where on the other hand the change of place is insignificant the scene division is indicated only by a space on the page. For ease of reference, however, the 'traditional' division is retained at the head of the page and in line numbering.

Notes. Passages on which there are notes are indicated by a † in the margin.

Punctuation adheres more closely than has been usual to the 'Elizabethan' punctuation of the early texts. It is often therefore more indicative of the way in which the lines were to be delivered than of their syntactical construction.

Glossaries are arranged on a somewhat novel principle, not alphabetically, but in the order in which the words or phrases occur. The editor is much indebted to Mr J. N. Bryson for his collaboration in the preparation of the glossaries.

Preface

The Text.   The first appearance of the play in print was in quarto in 1609. It had the following title-page :—THE LATE, / And much admired Play, / Called / Pericles, Prince / of Tyre / With the true Relation of the whole Historie, / aduentures, and fortunes of the said Prince : / As also, / The no lesse strange, and worthy accidents, / in the Birth and Life, of his Daughter / MARIANA. / As it hath been diuers and sundry times acted by / his Maiesties Seruants, at the Globe on / the Banck-side. / By William Shakespeare. / Imprinted at London for *Henry Gosson*, and are / to be sold at the signe of the Sunne in / Pater-noster row, &c. / 1609. It is a thoroughly bad text. There is some mislineation ; a good deal of verse is (as in *King Lear*) printed as prose, some prose is printed as though it were verse ; there are frequent non-metrical lines, in which a word has evidently been omitted, and there is a good deal of mere corruption. But the errors suggest the blunders of a more than ordinarily careless compositor (or of a compositor working from more than ordinarily difficult copy) rather than the auditory errors of a reporter, or the errors of a too familiar, and so careless, transcriber. The play was evidently popular, since it ran through six quarto editions by 1635, but it was not included in the First Folio, and indeed had to wait for canonisation till the Third Folio, where it is definitely attributed to Shakespeare.

Date of Composition.   Even the approximate determination of this depends on the view we take of the relation between Wilkins' novel and the play. If the play to which Wilkins alludes was the play as we have it, then we must put Shakespeare's work back to 1607. If on the other hand we assume that Shakespeare was indebted to the novel, then we must advance his work to 1609 or late 1608. It should be noticed that there is a passage in III. i. 30-37 (*i.e.* in the accepted Shakespearean portion of the play) in which the verbal coincidence with Wilkins is beyond the reach of chance.

Authorship. The attribution of the Quarto, accepted by the Third Folio, had evidently not commended itself to Heminge and Condell. Indeed their failure to include a play so popular is surely in itself a tacit denial of the title-page of the Quartos. And hardly any editors since have accepted the attribution, though that some of the play is Shakespeare's most would agree. The play falls clearly into several sections. There are the ' Gower' passages and the dumb-shows; the first two acts; the bulk of the last three acts; and the brothel-scenes in the fourth act. There is a general agreement that Shakespeare had no share, or the smallest possible share, in the Gower passages and the first two acts, but that he wrote either the whole or at least much the greater part of the last three acts less the brothel-scenes. With this general allocation the instinct of readers will pretty certainly agree. The first two acts are written in verse which reaches a somewhat low level of competence, but is for the most part dull and mechanical, and does not sound like Shakespeare at any stage of his development. The last three acts, on the other hand, give us again and again the true Shakespearean ring, and the ring of Shakespeare's later manner. But I think that they also give one the feeling of Shakespeare in something of a hurry, so that the characteristic felicities are less frequent than in what one may take to be his more deliberate work. As to the brothel-scenes, opinions have differed widely and feeling has run high. Fleay's remarks are worth quoting :—" These scenes are totally unlike Shakespeare's in feeling in such matters. He would not have indulged in the morbid anatomy of such loathsome characters; he would have covered the ulcerous sores with a film of humour, if it were a necessary part of his moral surgery to treat them at all—and above all he would not have married Marina to a man whose acquaintance she had first made in a public brothel, to which *his* motives of resort were not recommendatory, however involuntary *her* sojourn there may have been. A still stronger argument is the omission of any allusion in the after-scenes to these." This is a curious mixture of sentimentality and sound criticism. The scenes are loathsome; therefore let us at all costs, as another critic phrases it, ' relieve ' Shakespeare of them. There is no end to the operation of this kind of piety, which would surely excise at once the Overdone-Pompey scenes of *Measure for Measure*, which are little less rancid. Shakespeare was a ' moral surgeon'; possibly, but he was also a practical playwright, and if these scenes would tell in the theatre I do not think that he would have hesitated about them. But do they ? Here Fleay might have put much more strongly the point which he implies; not only are the scenes not mentioned later, but as they stand they are barely organic ; as a method either of ' illustrating Marina's virginal purity ' or of introducing Lysimachus to her, they are surely intolerably clumsy. And I think also that when one compares them with the scenes in *Measure for Measure* with which they are regularly compared by those who support Shakespeare's authorship of them, one is struck by the justice of Fleay's other point (though without any consideration of moral surgery); even in *Measure for Measure* there are touches of humour, cold-blooded, dreary, and to modern taste unsavoury though it is;

but these scenes are utterly humourless. They do not read to me as un-Shakespearean, and I am not clear that any of his contemporaries could have written them with such economy and trenchancy; but if they are Shakespeare's they are his in his blackest mood of disillusioned realism, the mood of *Timon*.

As to the authorship of the recognisedly non-Shakespearean portions of the play conjecture seems a sterile occupation. The favourite claimants are Wilkins and Rowley; and even if their reputation were a matter of importance to anybody, I do not see that it would be seriously enhanced or lowered by the attribution. The connection of Wilkins with the play is undoubted, though what exactly the connection was is a matter of dispute. In 1608 Wilkins published a novel, *The Painful Aduentures of Pericles Prince of Tyre. Being the true History of the Play of Pericles, as it was lately presented by the worthy and ancient Poet Iohn Gower.* In an 'epistle' prefixed to this he says, "A poore infant of my braine comes naked unto you." It is an interesting illustration of the conscious or unconscious dishonesty of critics hotly supporting a thesis that it has been again and again stated that Wilkins refers to the *play* as 'a poore infant of his braine,' when he clearly does nothing of the sort, but is speaking of the novel. For all that he may easily have been responsible for the first two acts of the play. But if he were 'novelising' his own work one would have expected the verbal parallels to have been closer than and different from what in fact we find them to be. But the whole problem seems to me so obscure, and a solution of it, even if one could be arrived at, so inconsiderable in value, that an examination of its intricacies would be, I think, waste of time. It is at least a reasonable view that Shakespeare took an existing play, could not be bothered to do anything with its episodic first two acts, but wrote on to them the whole of the Marina-story of the last three acts.

Sources. Both Wilkins' novel and the play are based on Gower's story of *Appollinus, the Prince of Tyr*, in *Confessio Amantis*, and on a novel by Twine, *The Patterne of Painefull Adventures*.

Duration of Action. Daniel divides into fourteen days, with intervals of varying lengths for a variety of voyages, and one long interval between Acts III and IV of fourteen years. The whole action is so episodic that one need hardly trouble about exact determination of time. But Daniel makes one remark, which, though he does not develop it, is of some significance as to the problem of authorship. He says that "the play consists of *seven* acts, distinctly marked by the choruses." If we follow this up we find that the Shakespearean portion of the play, the last three acts, not only forms a coherent whole in itself, but also falls into the traditional five acts, brief though they are.

Criticism. *Swinburne.*[1]—It is of course inexplicable, but it is equally of course undeniable, that the mention of Shakespeare's *Pericles* would seem immediately and invariably to recall to a virtuous critical public of nice and nasty mind the prose portions of the fourth act, the whole of the prose portions of the fourth act, and nothing but the prose portions of the fourth act. To readers and writers of books who readily admit their ineligibility as members of a Society for the Suppression of Shakespeare or Rabelais, of Homer or the Bible, it will seem that the third and

---

[1] Reprinted by permission of the Publishers, W. Heinemann Ltd., from *A Study of Shakespeare.*

xi

fifth acts of this ill-fated and ill-famed play, and with them the poetical parts of the fourth act, are composed of metal incomparably more attractive. But the virtuous critic, after the alleged nature of the vulturine kind, would appear to have eyes and ears and nose for nothing else. . . .

But what now shall I say that may not be too pitifully unworthy of the glories and the beauties, the unsurpassable pathos and sublimity inwoven with the imperial texture of this very play ? the blood-red Tyrian purple of tragic maternal jealousy, which might seem to array it in a worthy attire of its Tyrian name ; the flower-soft loveliness of maiden lamentation over the flower-strewn seaside grave of Marina's old sea-tossed nurse, where I am unvirtuous enough (as virtue goes among moralists) to feel more at home and better at ease than in the atmosphere of her later lodging in Mitylene ? What, above all, shall be said of that storm above all storms ever raised in poetry, which ushered into a world of such wonders and strange chances the daughter of the wave-worn and world-wandering prince of Tyre ? Nothing but this perhaps, that it stands—or rather let me say that it blows and sounds and shines and rings and thunders and lightens as far ahead of all others as the burlesque sea-storm of Rabelais beyond all possible storms of comedy.

PERICLES, PRINCE OF TYRE

DRAMATIS PERSONÆ

ANTIOCHUS, *king of Antioch.*
PERICLES, *prince of Tyre.*
HELICANUS, } *two lords of Tyre.*
ESCANES,
SIMONIDES, *king of Pentapolis.*
CLEON, *governor of Tarsus.*
LYSIMACHUS, *governor of Mytilene.*
CERIMON, *a lord of Ephesus.*
THALIARD, *a lord of Antioch.*
PHILEMON, *servant to Cerimon.*
LEONINE, *servant to Dionyza.*
Marshal.
A Pandar.
BOULT, *his servant.*

The daughter of Antiochus.
DIONYZA, *wife to Cleon.*
THAISA, *daughter to Simonides.*
MARINA, *daughter to Pericles and Thaisa.*
LYCHORIDA, *nurse to Marina.*
A Bawd.

Lords, Knights, Gentlemen, Sailors, Pirates,
Fishermen, and Messengers.

DIANA.

GOWER, *as Chorus.*

SCENE : *Dispersedly in various countries*

PERICLES, PRINCE OF TYRE

Act First

Enter Gower

Before the palace of Antioch

Gow. To sing a song that old was sung,
From ashes ancient Gower is come,
Assuming man's infirmities,
To glad your ear, and please your eyes:
It hath been sung at festivals,
On ember-eves and holy-ales;
And lords and ladies in their lives
Have read it for restoratives:
The purchase is to make men glorious;
Et bonum quo antiquius, eo melius.   10
If you, born in these latter times,
When wit's more ripe, acccept my rhymes,
And that to hear an old man sing
May to your wishes pleasure bring,
I life would wish, and that I might
Waste it for you, like taper-light.
This Antioch, then, Antiochus the Great

1

Built up, this city, for his chiefest seat,
The fairest in all Syria :
I tell you what mine authors say :   20
This king unto him took a fere,
Who died, and left a female heir,
So buxom, blithe and full of face
As heaven had lent her all his grace ;
With whom the father liking took,
And her to incest did provoke :
Bad child, worse father, to entice his own
To evil should be done by none :
But custom what they did begin
Was with long use account'd no sin.   30
The beauty of this sinful dame
Made many princes thither frame,
To seek her as a bed-fellow,
In marriage-pleasures play-fellow :
Which to prevent, he made a law,
To keep her still, and men in awe,
That whoso ask'd her for his wife,
His riddle told not, lost his life :
So for her many a wight did die,
As yon grim looks do testify.   40
What now ensues, to the judgement of your eye
I give my cause, who best can justify.   *Exit*

SCENE I

Antioch.   A room in the palace

Enter Antiochus, Prince Pericles and Followers

Ant. Young prince of Tyre, you have at large receiv'd
 The danger of the task you undertake.

Per. I have, Antiochus, and, with a soul
 Embolden'd with the glory of her praise,
 Think death no hazard in this enterprise.

Ant. Bring in our daughter, clothed like a bride,
 Fit for embracements even of Jove himself;
 At whose conception, till Lucina reign'd,
 Nature this dowry gave; to glad her presence,
 The senate-house of planets all did sit,   10
 To knit in her their best perfections.

Music.   Enter Antiochus' Daughter

Per. See where she comes, apparell'd like the spring,
 Graces her subjects, and her thoughts the king
 Of every virtue gives renown to men!
 Her face the book of praises, where is read
 Nothing but curious pleasures, as from thence
 Sorrow were ever raz'd, and testy wrath
 Could never be her mild companion.
 You gods that made me man, and sway in love,

That have inflam'd desire in my breast,   20
To taste the fruit of yon celestial tree,
Or die in the adventure, be my helps,
As I am son and servant to your will,
To compass such a boundless happiness !

Ant. Prince Pericles,—

Per. That would be son to great Antiochus.

Ant. Before thee stands this fair Hesperides,   †
With golden fruit, but dangerous to be touch'd ;
For death-like dragons here affright thee hard :   †
Her face, like heaven, enticeth thee to view   30
Her countless glory, which desert must gain ;
And which, without desert, because thine eye
Presumes to reach, all the whole heap must die.
Yon sometimes famous princes, like thyself,
Drawn by report, adventurous by desire,
Tell thee, with speechless tongues, and semblance pale,
That without covering, save yon field of stars,
Here they stand martyrs, slain in Cupid's wars ;
And with dead cheeks advise thee to desist
For going on death's net, whom none resist.   40

Per. Antiochus, I thank thee, who hath taught
My frail mortality to know itself,
And by those fearful objects to prepare
This body, like to them, to what I must ;

For death remember'd should be like a mirror,
Who tells us life 's but breath, to trust it error :
I 'll make my will then, and, as sick men do,
Who know the world, see heaven, but feeling woe
Gripe not at earthly joys as erst they did,
So I bequeath a happy peace to you   50
And all good men, as every prince should do ;
My riches to the earth, from whence they came ;
But my unspotted fire of love to you.
(*to the Princess*) Thus ready for the way of life or death,
I wait the sharpest blow.

Ant. Scorning advice : read the conclusion then :
Which read and not expounded, 'tis decreed,
As these before thee thou thyself shalt bleed.

Dau. Of all 'say'd yet, mayst thou prove prosperous !
Of all 'say'd yet, I wish thee happiness !   60

Per. Like a bold champion I assume the lists,
Nor ask advice of any other thought
But faithfulness and courage.

                    He reads the riddle

        ' I am no viper, yet I feed
        On mother's flesh which did me breed.
        I sought a husband, in which labour
        I found that kindness in a father :
        He 's father, son, and husband mild ;

                    5

       I mother, wife ; and yet his child.

       How they may be, and yet in two,   70

       As you will live, resolve it you.'

(*aside*) Sharp physic is the last : but, O you powers,

That give heaven countless eyes to view men's acts,

Why cloud they not their sights perpetually,

If this be true, which makes me pale to read it ?

Fair glass of light, I lov'd you, and could still,

Were not this glorious casket stor'd with ill :

But I must tell you, now my thoughts revolt,

For he 's no man on whom perfections wait

That, knowing sin within, will touch the gate.   80

You 're a fair viol, and your sense the strings,

Who, finger'd to make man his lawful music,

Would draw heaven down and all the gods, to hearken ;

But being play'd upon before your time,

Hell only danceth at so harsh a chime.

Good sooth, I care not for you.

Ant. Prince Pericles, touch not, upon thy life,

       For that 's an article within our law,

       As dangerous as the rest.   Your time 's expir'd :

       Either expound now, or receive your sentence.   90

Per. Great king,

       Few love to hear the sins they love to act ;

       'Twould braid yourself too near for me to tell it.

Who has a book of all that monarchs do,
He's more secure to keep it shut than shown :
For vice repeated 's like the wandering wind,
Blows dust in others' eyes to spread itself ;
And yet the end of all is bought thus dear,
The breath is gone, and the sore eyes see clear
To stop the air would hurt them.   The blind mole casts   100
Copp'd hills towards heaven, to tell the earth is throng'd
By man's oppression ; and the poor worm doth die for 't.
Kings are earth's gods ; in vice, their law 's their will ;
And if Jove stray, who dares say Jove doth ill ?
It is enough you know ; and it is fit,
What being more known grows worse, to smother it.
All love the womb that their first being bred,
Then give my tongue like leave to love my head.
Ant. (*aside*) Heaven, that I had thy head !   He has found the meaning :
But I will gloze with him.—Young prince of Tyre,   110
Though by the tenour of our strict edict,
Your exposition misinterpreting,
We might proceed to cancel of your days ;
Yet hope, succeeding from so fair a tree

7

As your fair self, doth tune us otherwise :
Forty days longer we do respite you,
If by which time our secret be undone,
This mercy shows we 'll joy in such a son :
And until then your entertain shall be
As doth befit our honour and your worth.   120

Exeunt all but Pericles

Per. How courtesy would seem to cover sin,
When what is done is like an hypocrite,
The which is good in nothing but in sight !
If it be true that I interpret false,
Then were it certain you were not so bad,
As with foul incest to abuse your soul ;
Where now you 're both a father and a son,
By your untimely claspings with your child
(Which pleasure fits a husband, not a father),
And she an eater of her mother's flesh,   130
By the defiling of her parent's bed ;
And both like serpents are, who though they feed
On sweetest flowers, yet they poison breed.
Antioch, farewell ! for wisdom sees, those men
Blush not in actions blacker than the night,
Will shun no course to keep them from the light.
One sin, I know, another doth provoke ;
Murder 's as near to lust as flame to smoke :

Poison and treason are the hands of sin,
Ay, and the targets to put off the shame :   140
Then, lest my life be cropp'd to keep you clear,
By flight I 'll shun the danger which I fear.   *Exit*

Re-enter Antiochus

Ant. He hath found the meaning, for the which we mean
To have his head.
He must not live to trumpet forth my infamy,
Nor tell the world Antiochus doth sin
In such a loathed manner :
And therefore instantly this prince must die,
For by his fall my honour must keep high.
Who attends us there ?   150

Enter Thaliard

Tha. Doth your highness call ?
Ant. Thaliard,
You are of our chamber, and our mind partakes
Her private actions to your secrecy :
And for your faithfulness we will advance you.
Thaliard, behold, here 's poison, and here 's gold ;
We hate the prince of Tyre, and thou must kill him :
It fits thee not to ask the reason why :
Because we bid it.   Say, is it done ?
Tha.   My lord,
'Tis done.   160

9

*Ant.*Enough.

Enter a Messenger

Let your breath cool yourself, telling your haste.

Mes. My lord, prince Pericles is fled.   *Exit*

Ant.   As thou

Wilt live, fly after : and like an arrow shot

From a well experienc'd archer hits the mark

His eye doth level at, so thou ne'er return

Unless thou say ' Prince Pericles is dead.'

Tha. My lord,

If I can get him within my pistol's length,

I 'll make him sure enough, so, farewell to your
highness,   170

Ant. Thaliard, adieu ! (*exit Thal.*)   Till Pericles be dead,

My heart can lend no succour to my head.   *Exit*

SCENE II

Tyre.   A room in the palace

Enter Pericles

Per. (*to Lords without*) Let none disturb us.   Why should
this change of thoughts,

The sad companion, dull-ey'd melancholy,

Be my so us'd a guest as not an hour,

10

In the day's glorious walk, or peaceful night,
The tomb where grief should sleep, can breed me
    quiet?
Here pleasures court mine eyes, and mine eyes shun
    them,
And danger, which I fear'd, is at Antioch,
Whose arm seems far too short to hit me here:
Yet neither pleasure's art can joy my spirits,
Nor yet the other's distance comfort me.   10
Then it is thus: the passions of the mind,
That have their first conception by mis-dread,
Have after-nourishment and life by care;
And what was first but fear what might be done,
Grows elder now, and cares it be not done.
And so with me: the great Antiochus,
'Gainst whom I am too little to contend,
Since he's so great, can make his will his act,
Will think me speaking, though I swear to silence,
Nor boots it me to say I honour him,   20
If he suspect I may dishonour him:
And what may make him blush in being known,
He'll stop the course by which it might be known:
With hostile forces he'll o'erspread the land,
And with the ostent of war will look so huge,
Amazement shall drive courage from the state,

11

  Our men be vanquish'd ere they do resist,
  And subjects punish'd that ne'er thought offence :
  Which care of them, not pity of myself,
  Who am no more but as the tops of trees   30
  Which fence the roots they grow by and defend them,
  Makes both my body pine, and soul to languish,
  And punish that before that he would punish.

    Enter Helicanus, with other Lords

1.*L.* Joy and all comfort in your sacred breast !

2.*L.* And keep your mind, till you return to us,
  Peaceful and comfortable !

Hel. Peace, peace, and give experience tongue.
  They do abuse the king that flatter him :
  For flattery is the bellows blows up sin ;
  The thing the which is flatter'd, but a spark,   40
  To which that blast gives heat and stronger glowing ;
  Whereas reproof, obedient and in order,
  Fits kings, as they are men, for they may err.
  When Signior Sooth here does proclaim a peace,
  He flatters you, makes war upon your life.
  Prince, pardon me, or strike me, if you please ;
  I cannot be much lower than my knees.

Per. All leave us else ; but let your cares o'erlook
  What shipping and what lading 's in our haven,
  And then return to us. (*exeunt Lords.*) Helicanus, thou 50

Hast mov'd us : what seest thou in our looks ?

Hel. An angry brow, dread lord.

Per. If there be such a dart in princes' frowns,
How durst thy tongue move anger to our face ?

Hel. How dare the plants look up to heaven, from whence
They have their nourishment ?

Per.   Thou know'st I have power
To take thy life from thee.

Hel. (*kneeling*) I have ground the axe myself ;
Do you but strike the blow.

Per. Rise, prithee, rise, sit down, thou art no flatterer :   60
I thank thee for it ; and heaven forbid
That kings should let their ears hear their faults hid !
Fit counsellor, and servant for a prince,
Who by thy wisdom makes a prince thy servant,
What wouldst thou have me do ?

Hel.   To bear with patience
Such griefs as you do lay upon yourself.

Per. Thou speak'st like a physician, Helicanus,
That ministers a potion unto me
That thou wouldst tremble to receive thyself.
Attend me then : I went to Antioch,   70
Where, as thou know'st, against the face of death,
I sought the purchase of a glorious beauty,
From whence an issue I might propagate,

13

Are arms to princes and bring joys to subjects.
Her face was to mine eye beyond all wonder;
The rest—hark in thine ear—as black as incest:
Which by my knowledge found, the sinful father
Seem'd not to strike, but smooth: but thou know'st
    this,
'Tis time to fear when tyrants seem to kiss.
Which fear so grew in me, I hither fled,   80
Under the covering of a careful night,
Who seem'd my good protector; and, being here,
Bethought me what was past, what might succeed.
I knew him tyrannous; and tyrants' fears
Decrease not, but grow faster than the years:
And should he doubt it, as no doubt he doth,
That I should open to the listening air
How many worthy princes' bloods were shed,
To keep his bed of blackness unlaid ope,
To lop that doubt, he 'll fill this land with arms,   90
And make pretence of wrong that I have done him;
When all, for mine, if I may call offence,
Must feel war's blow, who spares not innocence:
Which love to all, of which thyself art one,
Who now reprov'dst me for it,—

Hel.   Alas, sir !
Per. Drew sleep out of mine eyes, blood from my cheeks,

Musings into my mind, with thousand doubts
How I might stop this tempest ere it came ;
And finding little comfort to relieve them,
I thought it princely charity to grieve them.   100

Hel. Well, my lord, since you have given me leave to speak,
Freely will I speak.   Antiochus you fear,
And justly too, I think, you fear the tyrant,
Who either by public war or private treason
Will take away your life.
Therefore, my lord, go travel for a while,
Till that his rage and anger be forgot,
Or till the Fates do cut his thread of life.
Your rule direct to any ; if to me,
Day serves not light more faithful than I 'll be.   110

Per. I do not doubt thy faith ; but should he wrong
My liberties in my absence ?

Hel. We 'll mingle our bloods together in the earth,
From whence we had our being and our birth.

Per. Tyre, I now look from thee then, and to Tarsus
Intend my travel, where I 'll hear from thee,
And by whose letters I 'll dispose myself.
The care I had and have of subjects' good
On thee I lay, whose wisdom's strength can bear it.
I 'll take thy word for faith, not ask thine oath :   120
Who shuns not to break one will sure crack both :

But in our orbs we'll live so round and safe,
That time of both this truth shall ne'er convince,
Thou show'dst a subject's shine, I a true prince.

Exeunt

SCENE III

Tyre. An ante-chamber in the palace

Enter Thaliard

Tha. So, this is Tyre, and this the court. Here must I
kill King Pericles, and if I do it not, I am sure to be
hang'd at home: 'tis dangerous. Well, I perceive
he was a wise fellow, and had good discretion, that,
being bid to ask what he would of the king, desir'd
he might know none of his secrets: now I do see he
had some reason for 't; for if a king bid a man be a
villain, he's bound by the indenture of his oath to be
one. Hush! here come the lords of Tyre.

Enter Helicanus and Escanes, with other Lords

Hel. You shall not need, my fellow peers of Tyre,   10
Further to question me of your king's departure:
His seal'd commission left in trust with me
Doth speak sufficiently he's gone to travel.

Tha. (*aside*) How? the king gone?

Hel. If further yet you will be satisfied,

Why, as it were unlicens'd of your loves,
He would depart, I'll give some light unto you.
Being at Antioch—

Tha. (*aside*) What from Antioch?

Hel. Royal Antiochus—on what cause I know not—   20
Took some displeasure at him; at least he judg'd so:
And doubting lest that he had err'd or sinn'd,
To show his sorrow, he'ld correct himself;
So puts himself unto the shipman's toil,
With whom each minute threatens life or death.

Tha. (*aside*) Well, I perceive I shall not be hang'd now,
although I would; but since he's gone, the king's
seas must please: he 'scap'd the land, to perish at
the sea. I'll present myself. Peace to the lords of
Tyre!
                                                                                    30

Hel. Lord Thaliard from Antiochus is welcome.

Tha. From him I come
With message unto princely Pericles;
But since my landing I have understood
Your lord has betook himself to unknown travels;
Now message must return from whence it came.

Hel. We have no reason to desire it,
Commended to our master, not to us:
Yet, ere you shall depart, this we desire,
As friends to Antioch, we may feast in Tyre. *Exeunt* 40

17

SCENE IV

Tarsus. A room in the Governor's house

Enter Cleon the Governor of Tarsus, with Dionyza and others

Cle. My Dionyza, shall we rest us here,
And by relating tales of others' griefs,
See if 'twill teach us to forget our own?

Dio. That were to blow at fire in hope to quench it;
For who digs hills because they do aspire
Throws down one mountain to cast up a higher.
O my distressed lord, even such our griefs are;
Here they 're but felt, and seen with mischief's eyes,
But like to groves, being topp'd, they higher rise.

Cle. O Dionyza, 10
Who wanteth food, and will not say he wants it,
Or can conceal his hunger till he famish?
Our tongues and sorrows do sound deep
Our woes into the air; our eyes do weep,
Till tongues fetch breath that may proclaim them
louder;
That, if heaven slumber while their creatures want,
They may awake their helps to comfort them.
I 'll then discourse our woes, felt several years,

And wanting breath to speak help me with tears.

Dio. I'll do my best, sir.   20

Cle. This Tarsus, o'er which I have the government,
    A city on whom plenty held full hand,
    For riches strew'd herself even in the streets ;
    Whose towers bore heads so high they kiss'd the
        clouds,
    And strangers ne'er beheld but wonder'd at,
    Whose men and dames so jetted and adorn'd,
    Like one another's glass to trim them by :
    Their tables were stor'd full, to glad the sight,
    And not so much to feed on as delight ;
    All poverty was scorn'd, and pride so great,   30
    The name of help grew odious to repeat.

Dio. O, 'tis too true.

Cle. But see what heaven can do !   By this our change,
    These mouths, who but of late earth, sea and air,
    Were all too little to content and please,
    Although they gave their creatures in abundance,
    As houses are defil'd for want of use,
    They are now starv'd for want of exercise :
    Those palates who, not yet two summers younger,
    Must have inventions to delight the taste,   40
    Would now be glad of bread, and beg for it :
    Those mothers who, to nousle up their babes,

Thought nought too curious, are ready now
To eat those little darlings whom they lov'd.
So sharp are hunger's teeth, that man and wife
Draw lots who first shall die, to lengthen life :
Here stands a lord, and there a lady weeping ;
Here many sink, yet those which see them fall
Have scarce strength left to give them burial.
Is not this true ?   50

Dio. Our cheeks and hollow eyes do witness it.

Cle. O, let those cities that of plenty's cup
And her prosperities so largely taste,
With their superfluous riots, hear these tears !
The misery of Tarsus may be theirs.

Enter a Lord

Lo. Where 's the lord governor ?

Cle. Here.
Speak out thy sorrows which thou bring'st in haste,
For comfort is too far for us to expect.

Lo. We have descried, upon our neighbouring shore,   60
A portly sail of ships make hitherward.

Cle. I thought as much.
One sorrow never comes but brings an heir,
That may succeed as his inheritor ;
And so in ours : some neighbouring nation,
Taking advantage of our misery,

      Hath stuff'd the hollow vessels with their power,

      To beat us down, the which are down already,

      And make a conquest of unhappy me,

      Whereas no glory's got to overcome.   70

Lo. That's the least fear ; for, by the semblance,

      Of their white flags display'd, they bring us peace,

      And come to us as favourers, not as foes.

Cle. Thou speak'st like him's untutor'd to repeat :

      Who makes the fairest show means most deceit.

      But bring they what they will and what they can,

      What need we fear ?

      The ground's the lowest, and we are half way there.

      Go tell their general we attend him here,

      To know for what he comes, and whence he comes,   80

      And what he craves.

Lo. I go, my lord.   *Exit*

Cle. Welcome is peace, if he on peace consist ;

      If wars, we are unable to resist.

          Enter Pericles with Attendants

Per. Lord governor, for so we hear you are,

      Let not our ships and number of our men

      Be like a beacon fir'd, to amaze your eyes.

      We have heard your miseries as far as Tyre,

      And seen the desolation of your streets,

      Nor come we to add sorrow to your tears,   90

                     21

But to relieve them of their heavy load;
And these our ships, you happily may think
Are like the Trojan horse, was stuff'd within
With bloody veins expecting overthrow,
Are stor'd with corn to make your needy bread,
And give them life whom hunger starv'd half dead.

All. The gods of Greece protect you!
And we'll pray for you.

Per.   Arise, I pray you, rise:
We do not look for reverence, but for love
And harbourage for ourself, our ships and men.   100

Cle. The which when any shall not gratify,
Or pay you with unthankfulness in thought,
Be it our wives, our children, or ourselves,
The curse of heaven and men succeed their evils!
Till when,—the which I hope shall ne'er be seen—
Your grace is welcome to our town and us.

Per. Which welcome we'll accept; feast here awhile,
Until our stars that frown lend us a smile.   *Exeunt*

Act Second

Enter Gower

Gow. Here have you seen a mighty king
His child, I wis, to incest bring ;
A better prince and benign lord,
That will prove awful both in deed and word.
Be quiet then as men should be,
Till he hath pass'd necessity.
I 'll show you those in troubles reign,
Losing a mite, a mountain gain.
The good in conversation,
To whom I give my benison,   10
Is still at Tarsus, where each man
Thinks all is writ he speken can ;
And, to remember what he does,
Build his statue to make him glorious :
But tidings to the contrary
Are brought your eyes ; what need speak I ?

DUMB SHOW

*Enter, at one door, Pericles, talking with Cleon, all the train
with them.   Enter, at another door, a Gentleman, with a*

23

letter to Pericles, Pericles shows the letter to Cleon ; gives the Messenger a reward, and knights him. Exit Pericles at one door, and Cleon at another.

Good Helicane, that stay'd at home,
Not to eat honey like a drone
From others' labours ; though he strive
To killen bad, keep good alive ;   20
And to fulfil his prince' desire,
Sends word of all that haps in Tyre :
How Thaliard came full bent with sin
And had intent to murder him ;
And that in Tarsus was not best
Longer for him to make his rest.
He, doing so, put forth to seas,
Where when men been, there 's seldom ease ;
For now the wind begins to blow ;
Thunder above and deeps below   30
Make such unquiet that the ship
Should house him safe is wreck'd and split ;
And he, good prince, having all lost,
By waves from coast to coast is tost :
All perishen of man, of pelf,
Ne aught escapen but himself ;
Till fortune, tir'd with doing bad,

Threw him ashore, to give him glad :
And here he comes.   What shall be next,
Pardon old Gower,—this longs the text.   *Exit* 40

SCENE I

Pentapolis.   An open place by the sea-side

Enter Pericles, wet

Per. Yet cease your ire, you angry stars of heaven !
Wind, rain, and thunder, remember, earthly man
Is but a substance that must yield to you ;
And I, as fits my nature, do obey you :
Alas, the sea hath cast me on the rocks,
Wash'd me from shore to shore, and left me
        breath
Nothing to think on but ensuing death :
Let it suffice the greatness of your powers
To have bereft a prince of all his fortunes ;
And having thrown him from your watery grave,   10
Here to have death in peace is all he 'll crave.

Enter three Fishermen

1.*F.* What, ho, Pilch !
2.*F.* Ha, come and bring away the nets !

25

1.*F.* What, Patchbreech, I say!

3.*F.* What say you, master?

1.*F.* Look how thou stirrest now! come away, or I'll fetch thee with a wanion.

3.*F.* Faith, master, I am thinking of the poor men that were cast away before us even now.

1.*F.* Alas, poor souls, it grieved my heart to hear what   20
pitiful cries they made to us to help them, when, well-a-day, we could scarce help ourselves.

3.*F.* Nay, master, said not I as much when I saw the porpoise, how he bounc'd and tumbled? they say they're half fish, half flesh: a plague on them, they ne'er come but I look to be wash'd. Master, I marvel how the fishes live in the sea.

1.*F.* Why, as men do a-land; the great ones eat up the little ones: I can compare our rich misers to nothing so fitly as to a whale; a' plays and tumbles, driving   30
the poor fry before him, and at last devours them all at a mouthful: such whales have I heard on o' the land, who never leave gaping till they've swallow'd the whole parish, church, steeple, bells, and all.

Per. (*aside*) A pretty moral.

3.*F.* But, master, if I had been the sexton,
I would have been that day in the belfry.

2.*F.* Why, man?

3.*F.* Because he should have swallowed me too: and 40
when I had been in his belly, I would have kept
such a jangling of the bells, that he should never
have left till he cast bells, steeple, church, and
parish, up again.   But if the good King Simonides
were of my mind,—

Per. (*aside*) Simonides?

3.*F.* We would purge the land of these drones, that rob
the bee of her honey.

Per. (*aside*) How from the finny subject of the sea
These fishers tell the infirmities of men;
And from their watery empire recollect   50
All that may men approve or men detect!—
Peace be at your labour, honest fishermen.   †

2.*F.* Honest! good fellow, what's that?   If it be a day
fits you, search out of the calendar, and nobody look
after it.

Per. May see the sea hath cast upon your coast.

2.*F.* What a drunken knave was the sea to cast thee in
our way!

Per. A man whom both the waters and the wind,   60
In that vast tennis-court, have made the ball
For them to play upon, entreats you pity him;
He asks of you, that never us'd to beg.

27

1.*F.* No, friend, cannot you beg? Here's them in our
country of Greece gets more with begging than we
can do with working.

2.*F.* Canst thou catch any fishes then?

Per. I never practis'd it.

2.*F.* Nay, then thou wilt starve, sure; for here's nothing
to be got now-a-days, unless thou canst fish for 't.　70

Per. What I have been I have forgot to know:
But what I am, want teaches me to think on:
A man throng'd up with cold: my veins are chill, 　†
And have no more of life than may suffice
To give my tongue that heat to ask your help;
Which if you shall refuse, when I am dead,
For that I am a man, pray see me buried.

1.*F.* Die, quoth-a? Now gods forbid 't! And I have
a gown here, come, put it on, keep thee warm.
Now, afore me, a handsome fellow! Come, thou 　80
shalt go home, and we'll have flesh for holidays,
fish for fasting-days, and moreo'er puddings and
flap-jacks, and thou shalt be welcome.

Per. I thank you, sir.

2.*F.* Hark you, my friend; you said you could not beg?

Per. I did but crave.

2.*F.* But crave? Then I'll turn craver too, and so I
shall 'scape whipping.

Per. Why, are all your beggars whipped then?

2.*F.* O, not all, my friend, not all; for if all your beggars   90
were whipped, I would wish no better office than to
be beadle.   But, master, I'll go draw up the net.

Exit with Third Fisherman

Per. (*aside*) How well this honest mirth becomes their
labour!

1.*F.* Hark you, sir, do you know where ye are?

Per. Not well.

1.*F.* Why, I'll tell you: this is called Pentapolis, and
our king the good Simonides.

Per. The good Simonides, do you call him?

1.*F.* Ay, sir; and he deserves so to be called for his
peaceable reign and good government.   100

Per. He is a happy king, since he gains from his subjects
the name of good by his government.   How far is
his court distant from this shore?

1.*F.* Marry, sir, half a day's journey: and I'll tell you,
he hath a fair daughter, and to-morrow is her birth-
day; and there are princes and knights come from all
parts of the world to just and tourney for her love.

Per. Were my fortunes equal to my desires, I could wish
to make one there.

1.*F.* O, sir, things must be as they may; and what a man   110
cannot get, he may lawfully deal for his wife's soul.

Re-enter Second and Third Fishermen, drawing up a net

2.F. Help, master, help! here's a fish hangs in the net,
    like a poor man's right in the law; 'twill hardly come
    out. Ha! bots on't, 'tis come at last, and 'tis
    turn'd to a rusty armour.

Per. An armour, friends? I pray you, let me see it.
    Thanks, fortune, yet, that after all thy crosses
    Thou givest me somewhat to repair myself;
    And though it was mine own, part of my heritage,
    Which my dead father did bequeath to me,   120
    With this strict charge, even as he left his life,
    ' Keep it, my Pericles; it hath been a shield
    'Twixt me and death:'—and pointed to this brace—
    ' For that it sav'd me, keep it; in like necessity—
    The which the gods protect thee from!—may defend †
      thee.'
    It kept where I kept, I so dearly lov'd it,
    Till the rough seas, that spare not any man,
    Took it in rage, though calm'd have given 't again:
    I thank thee for 't, my shipwreck now 's no ill,
    Since I have here my father gave in 's will.   †

1.F. What mean you, sir?   131

Per. To beg of you, kind friends, this coat of worth,
    For it was sometime target to a king;
    I know it by this mark. He lov'd me dearly,

And for his sake I wish the having of it ;
And that you 'ld guide me to your sovereign's court,
Where with it I may appear a gentleman ;
And if that ever my low fortune 's better,
I 'll pay your bounties ; till then rest your debtor.

1.F. Why, wilt thou tourney for the lady ?   140

Per. I 'll show the virtue I have borne in arms.

1.F. Why, do 'e take it, and the gods give thee good on 't !

2.F. Ay, but hark you, my friend ; 'twas we that made
up this garment through the rough seams of the
waters : there are certain condolements, certain vails.
I hope, sir, if you thrive, you 'll remember from
whence you had them.

Per. Believe 't, I will.
By your furtherance I am cloth'd in steel ;
And spite of all the rapture of the sea   150
This jewel holds his building on my arm :
Unto thy value I will mount myself
Upon a courser, whose delightful steps
Shall make the gazer joy to see him tread.
Only, my friend, I yet am unprovided
Of a pair of bases.

2.F. We 'll sure provide : thou shalt have my best gown
to make thee a pair ; and I 'll bring thee to the court
myself.

Per. Then honour be but a goal to my will,   160
　　This day I'll rise, or else add ill to ill.   *Exeunt*

SCENE II

The same. A public way or platform leading to the lists. A
*   pavilion by the side of it for the reception of the King,*
*   Princess, Lords, &c.*

　　Enter Simonides, Thaisa, Lords, and Attendants

Sim. Are the knights ready to begin the triumph?
1.*L.* They are, my liege,
　　And stay your coming to present themselves.
Sim. Return them, we are ready; and our daughter,
　　In honour of whose birth these triumphs are,
　　Sits here, like beauty's child, whom nature gat
　　For men to see, and seeing wonder at.   *Exit a Lord*
Tha. It pleaseth you, my royal father, to express
　　My commendations great, whose merit's less.
Sim. It's fit it should be so, for princes are   10
　　A model which heaven makes like to itself:
　　As jewels lose their glory, if neglected,
　　So princes their renowns, if not respected.
　　'Tis now your honour, daughter, to entertain
　　The labour of each knight in his device.

Tha. Which, to preserve mine honour, I 'll perform.

    Enter a Knight ; he passes over, and his Squire presents
        his shield to the Princess

Sim. Who is the first that doth prefer himself ?

Tha. A knight of Sparta, my renowned father ;
    And the device he bears upon his shield
    Is a black Ethiope reaching at the sun ;
    The word, ' Lux tua vita mihi.'   20

Sim. He loves you well that holds his life of you.

                    The Second Knight passes

    Who is the second that presents himself ?

Tha. A prince of Macedon, my royal father ;
    And the device he bears upon his shield
    Is an arm'd knight that 's conquer'd by a lady ;
    The motto thus, in Spanish, ' Piu por dulzura que por
        fuerza.'   *The Third Knight passes*

Sim. And what 's the third ?

Tha.   The third of Antioch ;
    And his device, a wreath of chivalry ;
    The word, ' Me pompæ provexit apex.'   30

                    The Fourth Knight passes

Sim. What is the fourth ?

Tha. A burning torch that 's turned upside down ;
    The word, ' Quod me alit, me extinguit.'

Sim. Which shows that beauty hath his power and will,

Which can as well inflame as it can kill.

The Fifth Knight passes

Tha. The fifth, an hand environed with clouds,
Holding out gold that 's by the touchstone tried ;
The motto thus, ' Sic spectanda fides.'

The Sixth Knight, Pericles, passes

Sim. And what 's
The sixth and last, the which the knight himself   40
With such a graceful courtesy deliver'd ?

Tha. He seems to be a stranger ; but his present is
A wither'd branch, that 's only green at top ;
The motto, ' In hac spe vivo.'

Sim. A pretty moral ;
From the dejected state wherein he is,
He hopes by you his fortunes yet may flourish.

1.L. He had need mean better than his outward show
Can any way speak in his just commend ;
For by his rusty outside he appears   50
To have practised more the whipstock than the lance.

2.L. He well may be a stranger, for he comes
To an honour'd triumph strangely furnished.

3.L. And on set purpose let his armour rust
Until this day, to scour it in the dust.

Sim. Opinion 's but a fool, that makes us scan
The outward habit by the inward man.

But stay, the knights are coming : we will withdraw
Into the gallery.   *Exeunt*

    Great shouts within, and all cry ' The mean knight ! '

SCENE III

The same.   A hall of state : a banquet prepared

Enter Simonides, Thaisa, Lords, Knights, and Attendants

Sim. Knights,
    To say you 're welcome were superfluous.
    To place upon the volume of your deeds,
    As in a title-page, your worth in arms,
    Were more than you expect, or more than 's fit,
    Since every worth in show commends itself.
    Prepare for mirth, for mirth becomes a feast :
    You are princes and my guests.

Tha. But you, my knight and guest,
    To whom this wreath of victory I give,   **10**
    And crown you king of this day's happiness.

Per. 'Tis more by fortune, lady, than my merit.

Sim. Call it by what you will, the day is yours ;
    And here, I hope, is none that envies it.
    In framing an artist, art hath thus decreed,
    To make some good, but others to exceed,

And you are her labour'd scholar.   Come, queen o'
    the feast,—

For, daughter, so you are,—here take your place :

Marshal the rest as they deserve their grace.

Knights. We are honour'd much by good Simonides.   20

Sim. Your presence glads our days : honour we love ;

For who hates honour hates the gods above.

Mar. Sir, yonder is your place.

Per.   Some other is more fit.

1.K. Contend not, sir ; for we are gentlemen

That neither in our hearts nor outward eyes

Envy the great nor do the low despise.

Per. You are right courteous knights.

Sim.   Sit, sir, sit.

    (aside) By Jove, I wonder, that is king of thoughts,

These cates resist me, he but thought upon.

Tha. (aside) By Juno, that is queen of marriage,   30

All viands that I eat do seem unsavoury,

Wishing him my meat.—Sure he 's a gallant gentle-
    man.

Sim. He 's but a country gentleman ;

Has done no more than other knights have done ;

Has broken a staff or so ; so let it pass.

Tha. (aside) To me he seems like diamond to glass.

Per. (aside) Yon king 's to me like to my father's picture,

Which tells me in that glory once he was ;
Had princes sit like stars about his throne,
And he the sun, for them to reverence ;   40
None but beheld him but, like lesser lights,
Did vail their crowns to his supremacy :
Where now his son 's like a glow-worm in the night,
The which hath fire in darkness, none in light :
Whereby I see that Time 's the king of men ;
He 's both their parent, and he is their grave,
And gives them what he will, not what they crave.

Sim. What, are you merry, knights ?

Knights. Who can be other in this royal presence ?

Sim. Here, with a cup that 's stor'd unto the brim,   50
As you do love, fill to your mistress' lips,
We drink this health to you.

Knights.   We thank your grace.

Sim. Yet pause awhile :
Yon knight doth sit too melancholy,
As if the entertainment in our court
Had not a show might countervail his worth.
Note it not you, Thaisa ?

Tha. What is it to me, my father ?

Sim. O, attend, my daughter :
Princes, in this, should live like gods above,   60
Who freely give to every one that comes

37

To honour them :
And princes not doing so are like to gnats,
Which make a sound, but kill'd are wonder'd at.
Therefore to make his entrance more sweet,
Here, say we drink this standing-bowl of wine to him.

Tha. Alas, my father, it befits not me
Unto a stranger knight to be so bold :
He may my proffer take for an offence,
Since men take women's gifts for impudence.   70

Sim. How ?
Do as I bid you, or you 'll move me else.

Tha. (*aside*) Now, by the gods, he could not please me
        better.

Sim. And furthermore tell him, we desire to know of him,
Of whence he is, his name, and parentage.

Tha. The king my father, sir, has drunk to you.

Per. I thank him.

Tha. Wishing it so much blood unto your life.

Per. I thank both him and you, and pledge him freely.

Tha. And further he desires to know of you   80
Of whence you are, your name, and parentage.

Per. A gentleman of Tyre ; my name, Pericles ;
My education been in arts and arms ;
Who, looking for adventures in the world,
Was by the rough seas reft of ships and men,

And after shipwreck driven upon this shore.

Tha. He thanks your grace ; names himself Pericles,
A gentleman of Tyre,
Who only by misfortune of the seas
Bereft of ships and men, cast on this shore.   90

Sim. Now, by the gods, I pity his misfortune,
And will awake him from his melancholy.
Come, gentlemen, we sit too long on trifles,
And waste the time, which looks for other revels.
Even in your armours, as you are address'd,
Will very well become a soldier's dance.
I will not have excuse, with saying this
Loud music is too harsh for ladies' heads,
Since they love men in arms as well as beds.

The Knights dance

So, this was well ask'd, 'twas so well perform'd.   100
Come, sir,
Here's a lady that wants breathing too :
And I have heard, you knights of Tyre
Are excellent in making ladies trip,
And that their measures are as excellent.

Per. In those that practise them they are, my lord.

Sim. O, that's as much as you would be denied
Of your fair courtesy.   *The Knights and Ladies dance*
Unclasp, unclasp :

39

Thanks, gentlemen, to all ; all have done well,

(*to Per.*) But you the best. Pages and lights, to
   conduct   110

These knights unto their several lodgings ! Yours, sir,

We have given order to be next our own.

Per. I am at your grace's pleasure.

Sim. Princes, it is too late to talk of love,

And that 's the mark I know you level at :

Therefore each one betake him to his rest ;

To-morrow all for speeding do their best.   *Exeunt*

SCENE IV

Tyre.   A room in the Governor's house

Enter Helicanus and Escanes

Hel. No, Escanes, know this of me,

Antiochus from incest lived not free :

For which, the most high gods not minding longer

To withhold the vengeance that they had in store,

Due to this heinous capital offence,

Even in the height and pride of all his glory,

When he was seated in a chariot

Of an inestimable value, and

His daughter with him,

40

A fire from heaven came, and shrivell'd up   10
Their bodies, even to loathing ; for they so stunk,
That all those eyes ador'd them ere their fall
Scorn now their hand should give them burial.

Esc. 'Twas very strange.

Hel.   And yet but justice ; for though
This king were great, his greatness was no guard
To bar heaven's shaft, but sin had his reward.

Esc. 'Tis very true.

Enter two or three Lords

1.*L.* See, not a man in private conference
Or council has respect with him but he.

2.*L.* It shall no longer grieve without reproof.   20

3.*L.* And curs'd be he that will not second it.

1.*L.* Follow me then.   Lord Helicane, a word.

Hel. With me ? and welcome : happy day, my lords.

1.*L.* Know that our griefs are risen to the top,
And now at length they overflow their banks.

Hel. Your griefs ? for what ? wrong not your prince you
     love.

1.*L.* Wrong not yourself, then, noble Helicane ;
But if the prince do live, let us salute him,
Or know what ground 's made happy by his breath.
If in the world he live, we 'll seek him out ;   30
If in his grave he rest, we 'll find him there ;

And be resolv'd he lives to govern us,
Or dead, give 's cause to mourn his funeral,
And leave us to our free election.

2.L. Whose death 's indeed the strongest in our censure:
And knowing this kingdom is without a head,—
Like goodly buildings left without a roof
Soon fall to ruin—your noble self,
That best know how to rule and how to reign,
We thus submit unto, our sovereign.   40

All. Live, noble Helicane !

Hel. For honour's cause, forbear your suffrages :
If that you love Prince Pericles, forbear.
Take I your wish, I leap into the sea,
Where 's hourly trouble for a minute's ease.
A twelvemonth longer yet let me entreat
You to forbear the absence of your king ;
If in which time expir'd he not return,
I shall with aged patience bear your yoke.
But if I cannot win you to this love,   50
Go search like nobles, like noble subjects,
And in your search spend your adventurous worth ;
Whom if you find and win unto return,
You shall like diamonds sit about his crown.

1.L. To wisdom he 's a fool that will not yield ;
And since Lord Helicane enjoineth us,

We with our travels will endeavour it.

Hel. Then you love us, we you, and we 'll clasp hands :
When peers thus knit, a kingdom ever stands.

Exeunt

SCENE V

Pentapolis.   A room in the palace

*Enter Simonides, reading a letter, at one door :
the Knights meet him*

1.K. Good morrow to the good Simonides.

Sim. Knights, from my daughter this I let you know,
That for this twelvemonth she 'll not undertake
A married life.
Her reason to herself is only known,
Which from her by no means can I get.

2.K. May we not get access to her, my lord ?

Sim. Faith, by no means ; she hath so strictly tied
Her to her chamber, that 'tis impossible.
One twelve moons more she 'll wear Diana's livery ;   **10**
This by the eye of Cynthia hath she vow'd,
And on her virgin honour will not break it.

3.K. Loath to bid farewell, we take our leaves.

Exeunt Knights

Sim. So,

> They are well dispatch'd ; now to my daughter's
>> letter :
> She tells me here, she 'll wed the stranger knight,
> Or never more to view nor day nor light.
> 'Tis well, mistress ; your choice agrees with mine ;
> I like that well : nay, how absolute she 's in 't,
> Not minding whether I dislike or no !   20
> Well, I do commend her choice ;
> And will no longer have it be delay'd.
> Soft ! here he comes : I must dissemble it.

Enter Pericles

Per. All fortune to the good Simonides !

Sim. To you as much, sir !   I am beholding to you
> For your sweet music this last night : I do
> Protest my ears were never better fed
> With such delightful pleasing harmony.

Per. It is your grace's pleasure to commend ;
> Not my desert.

Sim.   Sir, you are music's master.   30

Per. The worst of all her scholars, my good lord.

Sim. Let me ask you one thing : what do you think of
> my daughter, sir ?

Per. A most virtuous princess.

Sim. And she is fair too, is she not ?

Per. As a fair day in summer, wondrous fair.

Sim. Sir, my daughter thinks very well of you,
    Ay, so well, that you must be her master,
    And she will be your scholar : therefore look to it.

Per. I am unworthy for her schoolmaster.

Sim. She thinks not so ; peruse this writing else.   40

Per. (*aside*) What 's here ?
    A letter, that she loves the knight of Tyre !
    'Tis the king's subtilty to have my life.—
    O, seek not to entrap me, gracious lord,
    A stranger and distressed gentleman,
    That never aim'd so high to love your daughter,
    But bent all offices to honour her.

Sim. Thou hast bewitch'd my daughter, and thou art
    A villain.

Per. By the gods, I have not :   50
    Never did thought of mine levy offence ;
    Nor never did my actions yet commence
    A deed might gain her love or your displeasure.

Sim. Traitor, thou liest.

Per.   Traitor !

Sim.   Ay, traitor.

Per. Even in his throat, unless it be the king,
    That calls me traitor, I return the lie.

Sim. (*aside*) Now, by the gods, I do applaud his courage.

Per. My actions are as noble as my thoughts,
    That never relish'd of a base descent.
    I came unto your court for honour's cause,   60
    And not to be a rebel to her state ;
    And he that otherwise accounts of me,
    This sword shall prove he 's honour's enemy.

Sim. No ?
    Here comes my daughter, she can witness it.

             Enter Thaisa

Per. Then, as you are as virtuous as fair,
    Resolve your angry father, if my tongue
    Did e'er solicit, or my hand subscribe
    To any syllable that made love to you.

Tha. Why, sir, say if you had,   70
    Who takes offence at that would make me glad ?

Sim. Yea, mistress, are you so peremptory ?
    (aside) I am glad on 't with all my heart.—
    I 'll tame you ; I 'll bring you in subjection.
    Will you, not having my consent,
    Bestow your love and your affections
    Upon a stranger ?   *(aside)* who, for aught I know,
    May be, nor can I think the contrary,
    As great in blood as I myself.—
    Therefore hear you, mistress ; either frame   80
    Your will to mine,—and you, sir, hear you,

Either be rul'd by me, or I will make you—
Man and wife :
Nay, come, your hands and lips must seal it too
And being join'd, I 'll thus your hopes destroy ;
And for a further grief,—God give you joy !
What, are you both pleas'd ?

Tha.   Yes, if you love me, sir.

Per. Even as my life my blood that fosters it.

Sim. What, are you both agreed ?

Both. Yes, if 't please your majesty.   90

Sim. It pleaseth me so well, that I will see you wed ;
And then, with what haste you can, get you to bed.

                                        Exeunt

Act Third

Enter Gower

Gow. Now sleep y-slaked hath the rout ;
No din but snores the house about,
Made louder by the o'er-fed breast
Of this most pompous marriage-feast.
The cat, with eyne of burning coal,
Now couches 'fore the mouse's hole ;
And crickets sing at the oven's mouth,

Are the blither for their drouth.
Hymen hath brought the bride to bed,
Where, by the loss of maidenhead,   10
A babe is moulded.   Be attent,
And time that is so briefly spent
With your fine fancies quaintly eche:
What's dumb in show I'll plain with speech.

DUMB SHOW

Enter Pericles and Simonides at one door, with Attendants; a Messenger meets them, kneels, and gives Pericles a letter: Pericles shows it Simonides; the Lords kneel to the former.   Then enter Thaisa with child, with Lychorida, a nurse: the King shows her the letter; she rejoices: she and Pericles take leave of her father, and depart with Lychorida and their Attendants.   Then exeunt Simonides and the rest.

By many a dern and painful perch
Of Pericles the careful search,
By the four opposing coigns
Which the world together joins,
Is made with all due diligence
That horse and sail and high expense   20
Can stead the quest.   At last from Tyre,

48

Fame answering the most strange inquire,
To the court of King Simonides
Are letters brought, the tenour these :
Antiochus and his daughter dead,
The men of Tyrus on the head
Of Helicanus would set on
The crown of Tyre, but he will none :
The mutiny he there hastes t' oppress ;
Says to 'em, if King Pericles   30
Come not home in twice six moons,
He, obedient to their dooms,
Will take the crown.   The sum of this,
Brought hither to Pentapolis,
Y-ravished the regions round,
And every one with claps can sound,
' Our heir-apparent is a king !
Who dream'd, who thought of such a thing ? '
Brief, he must hence depart to Tyre :
His queen with child makes her desire—   40
Which who shall cross ?—along to go.
Omit we all their dole and woe :
Lychorida, her nurse, she takes,
And so to sea : their vessel shakes
On Neptune's billow ; half the flood
Hath their keel cut : but fortune's mood

Varies again ; the grisled north
Disgorges such a tempest forth,
That, as a duck for life that dives,
So up and down the poor ship drives :   50
The lady shrieks and well-a-near
Does fall in travail with her fear :
And what ensues in this fell storm
Shall for itself itself perform.
I nill relate, action may
Conveniently the rest convey ;
Which might not what by me is told.
In your imagination hold
This stage the ship, upon whose deck
The sea-tost Pericles appears to speak.   *Exit* 60

SCENE I

Enter Pericles, on shipboard

Per. Thou god of this great vast, rebuke these surges,
    Which wash both heaven and hell ; and thou, that hast
    Upon the winds command, bind them in brass,
    Having call'd them from the deep ! O, still
    Thy deafening dreadful thunders ; gently quench
    Thy nimble sulphurous flashes ! O, how, Lychorida,

How does my queen ?   Thou stormest venomously ;
Wilt thou spit all thyself ?   The seaman's whistle
Is as a whisper in the ears of death,
Unheard.   Lychorida !—Lucina, O   10
Divinest patroness and midwife gentle
To those that cry by night, convey thy deity
Aboard our dancing boat ; make swift the pangs
Of my queen's travails !   Now, Lychorida !

Enter Lychorida, with an Infant

Lyc. Here is a thing too young for such a place,
Who, if it had conceit, would die, as I
Am like to do : take in your arms this piece
Of your dead queen.

Per.   How, how, Lychorida ?

Lyc. Patience, good sir, do not assist the storm.
Here's all that is left living of your queen,   20
A little daughter : for the sake of it,
Be manly, and take comfort.

Per.   O you gods !
Why do you make us love your goodly gifts,
And snatch them straight away ?   We here below
Recall not what we give, and therein may
Use honour with you.

Lyc.   Patience, good sir,
Even for this charge.

Per.   Now, mild may be thy life !
     For a more blustrous birth had never babe :
     Quiet and gentle thy conditions, for
     Thou art the rudeliest welcome to this world   30
     That ever was prince's child.   Happy what follows !
     Thou hast as chiding a nativity
     As fire, air, water, earth and heaven can make,
     To herald thee from the womb : even at the first
     Thy loss is more than can thy portage quit,   †
     With all thou canst find here.   Now, the good gods
     Throw their best eyes upon 't !

                    Enter two Sailors

1.S. What courage, sir ?   God save you !
Per. Courage enough, I do not fear the flaw ;
     It hath done to me the worst.   Yet, for the love   40
     Of this poor infant, this fresh new sea-farer,
     I would it would be quiet.
1.S. Slack the bolins there !   Thou wilt not, wilt thou ? †
     Blow, and split thyself.
2.S. But sea-room, an the brine and cloudy billow kiss the
     moon, I care not.
1.S. Sir, your queen must overboard : the sea works
     high, the wind is loud, and will not lie till the ship
     be clear'd of the dead.
Per. That 's your superstition.   50

1.S. Pardon us, sir ; with us at sea it hath been still
     observed ; and we are strong in custom.   Therefore
     briefly yield her ; for she must overboard straight.

Per. As you think meet.   Most wretched queen !

Lyc. Here she lies, sir.

Per. A terrible childbed hast thou had, my dear ;
     No light, no fire : the unfriendly elements
     Forgot thee utterly, nor have I time
     To give thee hallow'd to thy grave, but straight
     Must cast thee, scarcely coffin'd, in the ooze ;   60
     Where, for a monument upon thy bones,
     And aye-remaining lamps, the belching whale
     And humming water must o'erwhelm thy corpse,
     Lying with simple shells.   O Lychorida,
     Bid Nestor bring me spices, ink and paper,
     My casket and my jewels ; and bid Nicander
     Bring me the satin coffer : lay the babe
     Upon the pillow : hie thee, whiles I say
     A priestly farewell to her : suddenly, woman.

                                Exit Lychorida

2.S. Sir, we have a chest beneath the hatches, caulked   70
     and bitumed ready.

Per. I thank thee.   Mariner, say what coast is this ?

2.S. We are near Tarsus.

Per. Thither, gentle mariner,

       Alter thy course for Tyre.   When canst thou reach it?

2.S. By break of day, if the wind cease.

Per. O, make for Tarsus!

       There will I visit Cleon, for the babe

       Cannot hold out to Tyrus: there I'll leave it

       At careful nursing.   Go thy ways, good mariner,   80

       I'll bring the body presently.   *Exeunt*

SCENE II

Ephesus.   A room in Cerimon's house

*Enter Cerimon, a Servant, and some Persons who have
been shipwrecked*

Cer. Philemon, ho!

Enter Philemon

Phi. Doth my lord call?

Cer. Get fire and meat for these poor men;

       'T has been a turbulent and stormy night.

Ser. I have been in many; but such a night as this

       Till now, I ne'er endur'd.

Cer. Your master will be dead ere you return;

       There's nothing can be minister'd to nature

       That can recover him. *(to Phil.)* Give this to the

         'pothecary,

And tell me how it works.   *Exeunt all but Cerimon*
                       Enter two Gentlemen

1.*G.*   Good morrow.   10
2.*G.* Good morrow to your lordship.
Cer.   Gentlemen,
  Why do you stir so early?
1.*G.* Sir,
  Our lodgings, standing bleak upon the sea
  Shook as the earth did quake;
  The very principals did seem to rend
  And all to topple: pure surprise and fear
  Made me to quit the house.
2.*G.* That is the cause we trouble you so early;
  'Tis not our husbandry.
Cer.   O, you say well.   20
1.*G.* But I much marvel that your lordship, having
  Rich tire about you, should at these early hours
  Shake off the golden slumber of repose.
  'Tis most strange,
  Nature should be so conversant with pain,
  Being thereto not compell'd.
Cer.   I hold it ever,
  Virtue and cunning were endowments greater
  Than nobleness and riches: careless heirs
  May the two latter darken and expend,

But immortality attends the former, 30
Making a man a god.   'Tis known, I ever
Have studied physic, through which secret art,
By turning o'er authorities, I have,
Together with my practice, made familiar
To me and to my aid the blest infusions
That dwell in vegetives, in metals, stones ;
And I can speak of the disturbances
That nature works, and of her cures ; which doth
    give me
A more content in course of true delight
Than to be thirsty after tottering honour,   . 40
Or tie my pleasure up in silken bags,   †
To please the fool and death.

2.*G.* Your honour has through Ephesus pour'd forth
Your charity, and hundreds call themselves
Your creatures, who by you have been restor'd :
And not your knowledge, your personal pain, but even
Your purse, still open, hath built Lord Cerimon
Such strong renown as time shall never. . . .

       Enter two or three Servants with a chest

1.*S.* So ; lift there.
Cer. What's that ? 50
1.*S.* Sir,
    Even now did the sea toss up upon our shore

This chest : 'tis of some wreck.

Cer. Set 't down, let 's look upon 't.

2.*G.* 'Tis like a coffin, sir.

Cer.   Whate'er it be,
'Tis wondrous heavy.   Wrench it open straight :
If the sea's stomach be o'ercharg'd with gold,
'Tis a good constraint of fortune it belches upon us.

2.*G.* 'Tis so, my lord.

Cer. How close 'tis caulk'd and bitum'd !   Did the sea   60
cast it up ?

1.*S.* I never saw so huge a billow, sir, as toss'd it upon
shore.

Cer.   Wrench it open :
Soft ! it smells most sweetly in my sense.

2.*G.* A delicate odour.

Cer. As ever hit my nostril.   So, up with it.
O you most potent gods ! what 's here ? a corse ?

1.*G.* Most strange !

Cer. Shrouded in cloth of state ; balmed and entreasured
With full bags of spices !   A passport too !   70
Apollo, perfect me in the characters !

                              Reads from a scroll

      ' Here I give to understand,
      If e'er this coffin drive a-land,
      I, King Pericles, have lost

This queen, worth all our mundane cost.
Who finds her, give her burying;
She was the daughter of a king:
Besides this treasure for a fee,
The gods requite his charity!'

If thou livest, Pericles, thou hast a heart   80
That even cracks for woe!   This chanc'd to-night.

2.G. Most likely, sir.

Cer.   Nay, certainly to-night;
For look how fresh she looks!   They were too rough
That threw her in the sea.   Make a fire within:
Fetch hither all my boxes in my closet.

Exit a servant

Death may usurp on nature many hours,
And yet the fire of life kindle again
The o'erpress'd spirits.   I heard of an Egyptian
That had nine hours lien dead,
Who was by good appliance recovered.   90

Re-enter a Servant, with boxes, napkins, and fire

Well said, well said; the fire and cloths.
The rough and woful music that we have,
Cause it to sound, beseech you.
The viol once more: how thou stirr'st, thou block!
The music there!   I pray you, give her air.
Gentlemen,

    This queen will live : nature awakes ; a warmth   †
    Breathes out of her : she hath not been entranc'd
    Above five hours : see how she 'gins to blow
    Into life's flower again !

1.G.   The heavens,   100
    Through you, increase our wonder, and set up
    Your fame for ever.

Cer.   She is alive ; behold,
    Her eyelids, cases to those heavenly jewels
    Which Pericles hath lost, begin to part
    Their fringes of bright gold : the diamonds
    Of a most praised water do appear
    To make the world twice rich.   Live,
    And make us weep to hear your fate, fair creature,
    Rare as you seem to be.

Tha.   O dear Diana,
    Where am I ?   Where 's my lord ?   What world is
        this ?   110

2.G. Is not this strange ?

1.G. Most rare.

Cer. Hush, my gentle neighbours !
    Lend me your hands ; to the next chamber bear her.
    Get linen : now this matter must be look'd to,
    For her relapse is mortal.   Come, come ;
    And Æsculapius guide us ! *Exeunt, carrying her away*

SCENE III

Tarsus. A room in the Governor's house

Enter Pericles, Cleon, Dionyza, and Lychorida with
Marina in her arms

Per. Most honour'd Cleon, I must needs be gone ;
My twelve months are expired, and Tyrus stands
In a litigious peace.   You, and your lady,
Take from my heart all thankfulness !   The gods
Make up the rest upon you !

Cle. Your shafts of fortune, though they hurt you mortally †
Yet glance full wanderingly on us.

Dio.   O your sweet queen !
That the strict fates had pleas'd you had brought
       her hither,
To have bless'd mine eyes with her !

Per.   We cannot but obey
The powers above us.   Could I rage and roar   10
As doth the sea she lies in, yet the end
Must be as 'tis.   My gentle babe Marina, whom,
For she was born at sea, I have named so, here
I charge your charity withal, leaving her
The infant of your care ; beseeching you
To give her princely training, that she may be

Manner'd as she is born.

Cle.   Fear not, my lord, but think
Your grace, that fed my country with your corn,
For which the people's prayers still fall upon you,
Must in your child be thought on.   If neglection   20
Should therein make me vile, the common body,
By you reliev'd, would force me to my duty :
But if to that my nature need a spur,
The gods revenge it upon me and mine,
To the end of generation !

Per.   I believe you ;
Your honour and your goodness teach me to 't,
Without your vows.   Till she be married, madam,
By bright Diana, whom we honour, all
Unscissar'd shall this hair of mine remain,
Though I show ill in 't.   So I take my leave.   30
Good madam, make me blessed in your care
In bringing up my child.

Dio.   I have one myself,
Who shall not be more dear to my respect
Than yours, my lord.

Per.   Madam, my thanks and prayers.

Cle. We 'll bring your grace e'en to the edge o' the
        shore,
Then give you up to the mask'd Neptune, and   †

The gentlest winds of heaven.

Per.   I will embrace
Your offer.   Come, dearest madam.   O, no tears,
Lychorida, no tears :
Look to your little mistress, on whose grace   40
You may depend hereafter.   Come, my lord.

Exeunt

SCENE IV

Ephesus.   A room in Cerimon's house

Enter Cerimon and Thaisa

Cer. Madam, this letter, and some certain jewels,
Lay with you in your coffer : which are
At your command.   Know you the character ?
Tha. It is my lord's.
That I was shipp'd at sea, I well remember,
Even on my eaning time ; but whether there   †
Delivered, by the holy gods,
I cannot rightly say.   But since King Pericles,
My wedded lord, I ne'er shall see again,
A vestal livery will I take me to,   10
And never more have joy.
Cer. Madam, if this you purpose as ye speak,
Diana's temple is not distant far,

Where you may abide till your date expire ;
Moreover, if you please, a niece of mine
Shall there attend you.

Tha. My recompense is thanks, that 's all ;
Yet my good will is great, though the gift small.

Exeunt

Act Fourth

Enter Gower

Gow. Imagine Pericles arriv'd at Tyre,
Welcom'd and settled to his own desire.
His woeful queen we leave at Ephesus,
Unto Diana there 's a votaress.
Now to Marina bend your mind,
Whom our fast-growing scene must find
At Tarsus, and by Cleon train'd
In music, letters, who hath gain'd
Of education all the grace,
Which makes her both the heart and place   10
Of general wonder.   But, alack,
That monster envy, oft the wrack
Of earned praise, Marina's life

Seeks to take off by treason's knife ;
And in this kind hath our Cleon
One daughter, and a wench full grown,
Even ripe for marriage rite ; this maid
Hight Philoten : and it is said
For certain in our story, she
Would ever with Marina be :   20
Be 't when she weav'd the sleided silk
With fingers long, small, white as milk,
Or when she would with sharp neeld wound
The cambric, which she made more sound
By hurting it, or when to the lute
She sung, and made the night-bird mute,
That still records with moan, or when
She would with rich and constant pen   †
Vail to her mistress Dian ; still
This Philoten contends in skill   30
With absolute Marina : so
With the dove of Paphos might the crow
Vie feathers white.   Marina gets
All praises, which are paid as debts,
And not as given.   This so darks
In Philoten all graceful marks,
That Cleon's wife, with envy rare,
A present murderer does prepare

For good Marina, that her daughter
Might stand peerless by this slaughter.   40
The sooner her vile thoughts to stead,
Lychorida, our nurse, is dead :
And cursed Dionyza hath
The pregnant instrument of wrath
Prest for this blow.   The unborn event
I do commend to your content :
Only I carry winged time
Post on the lame feet of my rhyme ;
Which never could I so convey,
Unless your thoughts went on my way.   50
Dionyza does appear,
With Leonine, a murderer.   *Exit*

SCENE I

Tarsus.   An open place near the sea-shore

Enter Dionyza with Leonine

Dio. Thy oath remember, thou hast sworn to do 't : 'tis †
but a blow, which never shall be known.   Thou
canst not do a thing in the world so soon to yield
thee so much profit : let not conscience, which is
but cold, inflaming love i' thy bosom, inflame too †

65

nicely, nor let pity, which even women have cast
off, melt thee, but be a soldier to thy purpose.

Leo. I will do 't ; but yet she is a goodly creature.

Dio. The fitter then the gods should have her. Here she
comes weeping for her only mistress' death. Thou †
art resolv'd ?   11

Leo. I am resolv'd.

      Enter Marina, with a basket of flowers

Mar. No, I will rob Tellus of her weed,
To strew thy green with flowers : the yellows, blues,
The purple violets, and marigolds,
Shall, as a carpet, hang upon thy grave,
While summer-days do last. Ay me, poor maid,
Born in a tempest, when my mother died,
This world to me is like a lasting storm,
Whirring me from my friends.   20

Dio. How now, Marina ? why do you keep alone ?
How chance my daughter is not with you ?
Do not consume your blood with sorrowing :
You have a nurse of me. Lord, how your favour 's
Changed with this unprofitable woe !
Come, give me your flowers, ere the sea mar it.
Walk with Leonine ; the air is quick there,
And it pierces and sharpens the stomach.
Come, Leonine, take her by the arm, walk with her.

Mar. No, I pray you ;   30
      I'll not bereave you of your servant.

Dio. Come, come ;
      I love the king your father and yourself
      With more than foreign heart.   We every day
      Expect him here : when he shall come, and find
      Our paragon to all reports thus blasted,
      He will repent the breadth of his great voyage ;
      Blame both my lord and me, that we have taken
      No care to your best courses.   Go, I pray you,
      Walk, and be cheerful once again, reserve   40
      That excellent complexion, which did steal
      The eyes of young and old.   Care not for me ;
      I can go home alone.

Mar.   Well, I will go ;
      But yet I have no desire to it.

Dio. Come, come, I know 'tis good for you.
      Walk half an hour, Leonine, at the least :
      Remember what I have said.

Leo.   I warrant you, madam.

Dio. I'll leave you, my sweet lady, for a while :
      Pray, walk softly, do not heat your blood :
      What ! I must have care of you.

Mar.   My thanks, sweet madam.   50

                                Exit Dionyza

      Is this wind westerly that blows ?

Leo.   South-west.

Mar. When I was born, the wind was north.

Leo.   Was 't so ?

Mar. My father, as nurse said, did never fear,
    But cried ' Good seamen ! ' to the sailors, galling
    His kingly hands, haling ropes ;
    And, clasping to the mast, endur'd a sea
    That almost burst the deck.

Leo. When was this ?

Mar. When I was born :
    Never was waves nor wind more violent ;   60
    And from the ladder-tackle washes off
    A canvas-climber. ' Ha ! ' says one, ' wilt out ? '   †
    And with a dropping industry they skip
    From stem to stern : the boatswain whistles, and
    The master calls and trebles their confusion.

Leo. Come, say your prayers.

Mar. What mean you ?

Leo. If you require a little space for prayer,
    I grant it : pray ; but be not tedious,
    For the gods are quick of ear, and I am sworn   70
    To do my work with haste.

Mar.   Why will you kill me ?

Leo. To satisfy my lady.

*Mar.*Why would she have me kill'd ?
    Now, as I can remember, by my troth,
    I never did her hurt in all my life :
    I never spake bad word, nor did ill turn
    To any living creature : believe me, la,
    I never kill'd a mouse, nor hurt a fly :
    I trod upon a worm against my will,   †
    But I wept for it. How have I offended,   80
    Wherein my death might yield her any profit,
    Or my life imply her any danger ?

Leo. My commission
    Is not to reason of the deed, but do't.

*Mar.*You will not do't for all the world, I hope.
    You are well favour'd, and your looks foreshow
    You have a gentle heart. I saw you lately,
    When you caught hurt in parting two that fought :
    Good sooth, it show'd well in you : do so now :
    Your lady seeks my life ; come you between,   90
    And save poor me, the weaker.

Leo.   I am sworn,
    And will dispatch.   *He seizes her*

             Enter Pirates

1.*P.* Hold, villain !   *Leonine runs away*

2.*P.* A prize ! a prize !

3.*P.* Half-part, mates, half-part.

Come let 's have her aboard suddenly.

Exeunt Pirates with Marina

Re-enter Leonine

Leo. These roguing thieves serve the great pirate Valdes ;
And they have seized Marina.   Let her go :
There 's no hope she 'll return.   I 'll swear she 's dead,
And thrown into the sea.   But I 'll see further :   100
Perhaps they will but please themselves upon her,
Not carry her aboard.   If she remain,
Whom they have ravish'd must by me be slain.

Exit

SCENE II

Mytilene.   A room in a brothel

Enter Pandar, Bawd, and Boult

Pan. Boult !

Bou. Sir ?

Pan. Search the market narrowly ; Mytilene is full of
gallants.   We lost too much money this mart by
being too wenchless.

Bawd. We were never so much out of creatures.   We
have but poor three, and they can do no more than
they can do, and they with continual action are even
as good as rotten.

70

Pan. Therefore let's have fresh ones, what'er we pay for   10
them.   If there be not a conscience to be us'd in
every trade, we shall never prosper.

Bawd. Thou sayest true ; 'tis not our bringing up of poor
bastards,—as, I think, I have brought up some
eleven—

Bou. Ay, to eleven ; and brought them down again.
But shall I search the market ?

Bawd. What else, man ?   The stuff we have, a strong
wind will blow it to pieces, they are so pitifully
sodden.   20

Pan. Thou sayest true ; they're too unwholesome, o'
conscience.   The poor Transylvanian is dead, that
lay with the little baggage.

Bou. Ay, she quickly poop'd him ; she made him roast-
meat for worms.   But I'll go search the market.

Exit

Pan. Three or four thousand chequins were as pretty a
proportion to live quietly, and so give over.

Bawd. Why to give over, I pray you ? is it a shame to get
when we are old ?

Pan. O, our credit comes not in like the commodity, nor   30
the commodity wages not with the danger : therefore, if in our youths we could pick up some pretty
estate, 'twere not amiss to keep our door hatch'd.

Besides, the sore terms we stand upon with the gods will be strong with us for giving o'er.

Bawd. Come, other sorts offend as well as we.

Pan. As well as we ! ay, and better too ; we offend worse. Neither is our profession any trade ; it 's no calling. But here comes Boult.

Re-enter Boult, with the Pirates and Marina

Bou. (to Mar.) Come your ways. My masters, you say   40
she 's a virgin ?

1.P. O, sir, we doubt it not.

Bou. Master, I have gone through for this piece you see : if you like her, so ; if not, I have lost my earnest.

Bawd. Boult, has she any qualities ?

Bou. She has a good face, speaks well, and has excellent good clothes : there 's no farther necessity of qualities can make her be refus'd.

Bawd. What 's her price, Boult ?

Bou. I cannot be bated one doit of a thousand pieces.   50

Pan. Well, follow me, my masters, you shall have your money presently. Wife, take her in, instruct her what she has to do, that she may not be raw in her entertainment.   *Exeunt Pandar and Pirates*

Bawd. Boult, take you the marks of her, the colour of her hair, complexion, height, her age, with warrant of her virginity ; and cry ' He that will give most

shall have her first.'   Such a maidenhead were no
cheap thing, if men were as they have been.   Get
this done as I command you.   60

Bou. Performance shall follow.   *Exit*

Mar. Alack that Leonine was so slack, so slow !
    He should have struck, not spoke ; or that these
        pirates,
    Not enough barbarous, had o'erboard thrown me
    For to seek my mother !

Bawd. Why lament you, pretty one ?

Mar. That I am pretty.

Bawd. Come, the gods have done their part in you.

Mar. I accuse them not.

Bawd. You are light into my hands, where you are like to   70
live.

Mar. The more my fault,
    To 'scape his hands where I was like to die.

Bawd. Ay, and you shall live in pleasure.

Mar. No.

Bawd. Yes, indeed shall you, and taste gentlemen of all
fashions, you shall fare well, you shall have the difference of all complexions.   What, do you stop your
ears ?

Mar. Are you a woman ?   80

Bawd. What would you have me be, an I be not a woman ?

73

Mar. An honest woman, or not a woman.

Bawd. Marry, whip thee, gosling : I think I shall have something to do with you. Come, you 're a young foolish sapling, and must be bow'd as I would have you.

Mar. The gods defend me !

Bawd. If it please the gods to defend you by men, then men must comfort you, men must feed you, men must stir you up. Boult 's returned. 90

Re-enter Boult

Now, sir, hast thou cried her through the market ?

Bou. I have cried her almost to the number of her hairs, I have drawn her picture with my voice.

Bawd. And I prithee tell me, how dost thou find the inclination of the people, especially of the younger sort ?

Bou. Faith, they listened to me as they would have hearkened to their father's testament ; there was a Spaniard's mouth so water'd, that he went to bed to her very description. 100

Bawd. We shall have him here to-morrow with his best ruff on.

Bou. To-night, to-night. But, mistress, do you know the French knight that cowers i' the hams ?

Bawd. Who, Monsieur Veroles ?

74

Bou. Ay, he : he offered to cut a caper at the proclamation,
but he made a groan at it, and swore he would see
her to-morrow.

Bawd. Well, well ; as for him, he brought his disease
hither ; here he does but repair it. I know he will   110
come in our shadow, to scatter his crowns in the sun.

Bou. Well, if we had of every nation a traveller, we should
lodge them with this sign.

Bawd. Pray you, come hither awhile ; you have fortunes
coming upon you ; mark me, you must seem to do
that fearfully which you commit willingly, despise
profit where you have most gain ; to weep that you
live as we do makes pity in your lovers, seldom but
that pity begets you a good opinion, and that opinion
a mere profit.   120

Mar. I understand you not.

Bou. O, take her home, mistress, take her home : these
blushes of hers must be quench'd with some present
practice.

Bawd. Thou sayest true, i' faith, so they must, for your
bride goes to that with shame which is her way to go
with warrant.

Bou. Faith, some do, and some do not. But, mistress, if
I have bargained for the joint,—

Bawd. Thou mayst cut a morsel off the spit.   130

PERICLES

Bou. I may so.

Bawd. Who should deny it? Come, young one, I like
the manner of your garments well.

Bou. Ay, by my faith, they shall not be chang'd yet.

Bawd. Boult, spend thou that in the town: report what
a sojourner we have, you 'll lose nothing by custom.
When nature fram'd this piece, she meant thee a good
turn; therefore say what a paragon she is, and thou
hast the harvest out of thine own report.

Bou. I warrant you, mistress, thunder shall not so awake 140
the beds of eels as my giving out her beauty stirs up
the lewdly-inclined. I 'll bring home some to-night.

Bawd. Come your ways; follow me.

Mar. If fires be hot, knives sharp, or waters deep,
Untied I still my virgin knot will keep.
Diana, aid my purpose!

Bawd. What have we to do with Diana? Pray you, will
you go with us?   *Exeunt*

SCENE III

Tarsus.   A room in the Governor's house

Enter Cleon and Dionyza

Dio. Why, are you foolish? Can it be undone?

Cle. O Dionyza, such a piece of slaughter

76

The sun and moon ne'er look'd upon !

Dio.   I think
You 'll turn a child again.

Cle. Were I chief lord of all this spacious world,
I 'ld give it to undo the deed.   O lady,
Much less in blood than virtue, yet a princess
To equal any single crown o' the earth
I' the justice of compare !   O villain Leonine !
Whom thou hast poison'd too :   10
If thou hadst drunk to him, 't had been a kindness
Becoming well thy fact : what canst thou say
When noble Pericles shall demand his child ?

Dio. That she is dead.   Nurses are not the fates,
To foster it, nor ever to preserve.
She died at night ; I 'll say so.   Who can cross it ?
Unless you play the pious innocent,
And for an honest attribute cry out
' She died by foul play.'

Cle.   O, go to.   Well, well,
Of all the faults beneath the heavens, the gods   20
Do like this worst.

Dio.   Be one of those that think
The pretty wrens of Tarsus will fly hence
And open this to Pericles.   I do shame
To think of what a noble strain you are

And of how coward a spirit.

Cle.   To such proceeding
Who ever but his approbation added,
Though not his prime consent, he did not flow
From honourable sources.

Dio.   Be it so, then :
Yet none does know, but you, how she came dead,
Nor none can know, Leonine being gone.   30
She did distain my child, and stood between
Her and her fortunes : none would look on her,
But cast their gazes on Marina's face ;
Whilst ours was blurted at, and held a malkin,
Not worth the time of day.   It pierc'd me thorough ;
And though you call my course unnatural,
You not your child well loving, yet I find
It greets me as an enterprise of kindness
Perform'd to your sole daughter.

Cle.   Heavens forgive it !

Dio. And as for Pericles,   40
What should he say ?   We wept after her hearse,
And yet we mourn : her monument
Is almost finish'd, and her epitaphs
In glittering golden characters express
A general praise to her, and care in us
At whose expense 'tis done.

Cle.   Thou art like the harpy, †
         Which, to betray, dost, with thine angel's face,
         Seize with thine eagle's talons.
Dio. You are like one that superstitiously
         Doth swear to the gods that winter kills the flies :   50
         But yet I know you 'll do as I advise.   *Exeunt*

SCENE IV

Enter Gower, before the monument of Marina at Tarsus

Gow. Thus time we waste, and longest leagues make short ;
         Sail seas in cockles, have and wish but for 't ;
         Making, to take our imagination,
         From bourn to bourn, region to region.
         By you being pardon'd, we commit no crime
         To use one language in each several clime
         Where our scenes seem to live.   I do beseech you
         To learn of me, who stand i' the gaps to teach you
         The stages of our story.   Pericles
         Is now again thwarting the wayward seas,   10
         Attended on by many a lord and knight,
         To see his daughter, all his life's delight.
         Old Helicanus goes along ; behind
         Is left to govern it, you bear in mind

Old Escanes, whom Helicanus late
Advanc'd in time to great and high estate.
Well-sailing ships and bounteous winds have brought
This king to Tarsus,—think this pilot thought :
So with his steerage shall your thoughts grow on,—
To fetch his daughter home, who first is gone.   20
Like motes and shadows see them move awhile ;
Your ears unto your eyes I 'll reconcile.

DUMB SHOW

*Enter Pericles at one door, with all his train ; Cleon and
Dionyza at the other.   Cleon shows Pericles the tomb ;
whereat Pericles makes lamentation, puts on sackcloth,
and in a mighty passion departs.   Then exeunt Cleon,
Dionyza, and the rest.*

See how belief may suffer by foul show !
This borrow'd passion stands for true old woe ;
And Pericles, in sorrow all devour'd,
With sighs shot through, and biggest tears o'er-
    shower'd,
Leaves Tarsus, and again embarks.   He swears
Never to wash his face, nor cut his hairs :
He puts on sackcloth, and to sea.   He bears
A tempest, which his mortal vessel tears,   30

And yet he rides it out.   Now please you wit
The epitaph is for Marina writ
By wicked Dionyza.

Reads the inscription on Marina's monument

' The fairest, sweet'st and best, lies here,
Who wither'd in her spring of year.
She was of Tyrus the king's daughter,
On whom foul death hath made this slaughter ;
Marina was she call'd ; and at her birth,
Thetis, being proud, swallow'd some part o' the earth :
Therefore the earth, fearing to be o'erflow'd :   40
Hath Thetis' birth-child on the heavens bestow'd :
Wherefore she does, and swears she 'll never stint,
Make raging battery upon shores of flint.'

No visor does become black villany
So well as soft and tender flattery.
Let Pericles believe his daughter 's dead,
And bear his courses to be ordered
By Lady Fortune, while our scene must play
His daughter's woe and heavy well-a-day
In her unholy service.   Patience, then,   50
And think you now are all in Mytilene.   *Exit*

SCENE V

Mytilene.   A street before the brothel

Enter, from the brothel, two Gentlemen

1.G. Did you ever hear the like?

2.G. No, nor never shall do in such a place as this, she
being once gone.

1.G. But to have divinity preach'd there, did you ever
dream of such a thing?

2.G. No, no.   Come, I am for no more bawdy-houses:
shall's go hear the vestals sing?

1.G. I'll do any thing now that is virtuous, but I am
out of the road of rutting for ever.   *Exeunt*

SCENE VI

The same.   A room in the brothel

Enter Pandar, Bawd, and Boult

Pan. Well, I had rather than twice the worth of her she
had ne'er come here.

Bawd. Fie, fie upon her! she's able to freeze the god
Priapus, and undo a whole generation.   We must
either get her ravish'd or be rid of her.   When she
should do for clients her fitment and do me the

kindness of our profession, she has me her quirks,
her reasons, her master reasons, her prayers, her
knees, that she would make a puritan of the devil,
if he should cheapen a kiss of her.   10

Bou. Faith, I must ravish her, or she 'll disfurnish us of
all our cavaliers and make our swearers priests.

Pan. Now, the pox upon her green-sickness for me !

Bawd. Faith, there 's no way to be rid on 't but by the
way to the pox.   Here comes the Lord Lysimachus
disguised.

Bou. We should have both lord and lown, if the peevish
baggage would but give way to customers.

Enter Lysimachus

Lys. How now, how a dozen of virginities ?

Bawd. Now, the gods to-bless your honour !   20

Bou. I am glad to see your honour in good health.

Lys. You may so ; 'tis the better for you that your
resorters stand upon sound legs. How now,
wholesome iniquity, have you that a man may deal
withal, and defy the surgeon ?

Bawd. We have here one, sir, if she would—but there
never came her like in Mytilene.

Lys. If she 'ld do the deed of darkness, thou wouldst say.

Bawd. Your honour knows what 'tis to say well enough.

Lys. Well, call forth, call forth.   30

Bou. For flesh and blood, sir, white and red, you shall
see a rose ; and she were a rose indeed, if she had
but—

Lys. What, prithee ?

Bou. O, sir, I can be modest.

Lys. That dignifies the renown of a bawd, no less than it
gives a good report to a number to be chaste.   †

Exit Boult

Bawd. Here comes that which grows to the stalk ; never
plucked yet, I can assure you.

Re-enter Boult with Marina

Is she not a fair creature ?   40

Lys. Faith, she would serve after a long voyage at sea.
Well, there 's for you : leave us.

Bawd. I beseech your honour, give me leave a word, and
I 'll have done presently.

Lys. I beseech you, do.

Bawd. (*to Marina*) First, I would have you note, this is
an honourable man.

Mar. I desire to find him so, that I may worthily note him.

Bawd. Next, he 's the governor of this country, and a
man whom I am bound to.   5

Mar. If he govern the country, you are bound to him
indeed, but how honourable he is in that, I know
not.

Bawd. Pray you, without any more virginal fencing, will
    you use him kindly? He will line your apron
    with gold.

Mar. What he will do graciously, I will thankfully receive.

Lys. Ha' you done?

Bawd. My lord, she's not pac'd yet: you must take
    some pains to work her to your manage. Come, 60
    we will leave his honour and her together. Go thy
    ways.   *Exeunt Bawd, Pandar, and Boult*

Lys. Now, pretty one, how long have you been at this
    trade?

Mar. What trade, sir?

Lys. Why, I cannot name 't but I shall offend.

Mar. I cannot be offended with my trade. Please you to
    name it.

Lys. How long have you been of this profession?

Mar. E'er since I can remember.   70

Lys. Did you go to it so young? Were you a gamester
    at five or at seven?

Mar. Earlier too, sir, if now I be one.

Lys. Why, the house you dwell in proclaims you to be a
    creature of sale.

Mar. Do you know this house to be a place of such resort,
    and will come into 't? I hear say you are of
    honourable parts and are the governor of this place.

Lys. Why, hath your principal made known unto you
    who I am?   80

Mar. Who is my principal?

Lys. Why, your herb-woman; she that sets seeds and
    roots of shame and iniquity. O, you have heard
    something of my power, and so stand aloof for
    more serious wooing. But I protest to thee, pretty
    one, my authority shall not see thee, or else look
    friendly upon thee. Come, bring me to some
    private place; come, come.

Mar. If you were born to honour, show it now;
    If put upon you, make the judgement good   90
    That thought you worthy of it.

Lys. How's this? how's this? Some more; be sage.

Mar.   For me
    That am a maid, though most ungentle fortune
    Have placed me in this sty, where, since I came,
    Diseases have been sold dearer than physic,
    O, that the gods
    Would set me free from this unhallow'd place,
    Though they did change me to the meanest bird
    That flies i' the purer air!

Lys.   I did not think
    Thou couldst have spoke so well; ne'er dream'd
    thou couldst.   100

Had I brought hither a corrupted mind,
Thy speech had alter'd it. Hold, here's gold for thee:
Persever in that clear way thou goest,
And the gods strengthen thee !

Mar.   The good gods preserve you !

Lys. For me, be you thoughten
That I came with no ill intent ; for to me
The very doors and windows savour vilely.
Fare thee well.   Thou art a piece of virtue, and
I doubt not but thy training hath been noble.
Hold, here's more gold for thee.   110
A curse upon him, die he like a thief,
That robs thee of thy goodness !   If thou dost
Hear from me, it shall be for thy good.

Re-enter Boult

Bou. I beseech your honour, one piece for me.

Lys. Avaunt, thou damned door-keeper !
Your house, but for this virgin that doth prop it,
Would sink, and overwhelm you.   Away !   *Exit*

Bou. How's this ?   We must take another course with
you.   If your peevish chastity, which is not worth
a breakfast in the cheapest country under the cope,   120
shall undo a whole household, let me be gelded like
a spaniel.   Come your ways.

Mar. Whither would you have me ?

Bou. I must have your maidenhead taken off, or the common hangman shall execute it. Come your ways. We'll have no more gentlemen driven away. Come your ways, I say.

Re-enter Bawd

Bawd. How now, what's the matter?

Bou. Worse and worse, mistress; she has here spoken holy words to the Lord Lysimachus.   130

Bawd. O abominable!

Bou. She makes our profession as it were to stink afore the face of the gods.

Bawd. Marry, hang her up for ever!

Bou. The nobleman would have dealt with her like a nobleman, and she sent him away as cold as a snow-ball, saying his prayers too.

Bawd. Boult, take her away, use her at thy pleasure, crack the glass of her virginity, and make the rest malleable.

Bou. An if she were a thornier piece of ground than she 140 is, she shall be ploughed.

Mar. Hark, hark, you gods!

Bawd. She conjures, away with her! Would she had never come within my doors! Marry, hang you! She's born to undo us. Will you not go the way of women-kind? Marry, come up, my dish of chastity with rosemary and bays!   *Exit*

Bou. Come, mistress, come your ways with me.

Mar. Whither wilt thou have me ?

Bou. To take from you the jewel you hold so dear.   150

Mar. Prithee, tell me one thing first.

Bou. Come now, your one thing.

Mar. What canst thou wish thine enemy to be ?

Bou. Why, I could wish him to be my master, or rather,
    my mistress.

Mar. Neither of these are so bad as thou art,
    Since they do better thee in their command.
    Thou hold'st a place, for which the pained'st fiend
    Of hell would not in reputation change :
    Thou art the damned door-keeper to every   160
    Coistrel that comes inquiring for his Tib ;
    To the choleric fisting of every rogue
    Thy ear is liable ; thy food is such
    As hath been belch'd on by infected lungs.

Bou. What would you have me do ? go to the wars, would
    you ? where a man may serve seven years for the loss
    of a leg, and have not money enough in the end to
    buy him a wooden one ?

Mar. Do any thing but this thou doest.   Empty
    Old receptacles, or common shores, of filth ;   170
    Serve by indenture to the common hangman :
    Any of these ways are yet better than this ;

For what thou professest, a baboon, could he speak,
Would own a name too dear.   O, that the gods
Would safely deliver me from this place !
Here, here's gold for thee.
If that thy master would gain by me,
Proclaim that I can sing, weave, sew, and dance,
With other virtues, which I'll keep from boast ;
And I will undertake all these to teach.   180
I doubt not but this populous city will
Yield many scholars.

Bou. But can you teach all this you speak of ?

Mar. Prove that I cannot, take me home again,
And prostitute me to the basest groom
That doth frequent your house.

Bou. Well, I will see what I can do for thee : if I can
place thee, I will.

Mar. But amongst honest women.

Bou. Faith, my acquaintance lies little amongst them. 190
But since my master and mistress have bought you,
there's no going but by their consent : therefore I
will make them acquainted with your purpose, and
I doubt not but I shall find them tractable enough.
Come, I'll do for thee what I can ; come your ways.

Exeunt

Act Fifth

Enter Gower

Gow. Marina thus the brothel 'scapes, and chances
    Into an honest house, our story says.
She sings like one immortal, and she dances
    As goddess-like to her admired lays ;
Deep clerks she dumbs, and with her needle
    composes
    Nature's own shape, of bud, bird, branch, or
    berry,
That even her art sisters the natural roses ;
    Her inkle, silk, twin with the rubied cherry :
That pupils lacks she none of noble race,
    Who pour their bounty on her, and her gain   10
She gives the cursed bawd. Here we her place ;
    And to her father turn our thoughts again,
Where we left him, on the sea. We there him lost :
    Whence, driven before the winds, he is arriv'd
Here where his daughter dwells, and on this coast
    Suppose him now at anchor. The city 's hiv'd   †
God Neptune's annual feast to keep : from whence
    Lysimachus our Tyrian ship espies,

91

His banners sable, trimm'd with rich expense ;
   And to him in his barge with fervour hies.   20
In your supposing once more put your sight
   Of heavy Pericles ; think this his bark :
Where what is done in action, more, if might,   †
   Shall be discover'd ; please you, sit, and hark.

                              Exit

SCENE I

*On board Pericles' ship, off Mytilene. A close pavilion on
deck, with a curtain before it ; Pericles within it, reclined
on a couch. A barge lying beside the Tyrian vessel*

*Enter two sailors, one belonging to the Tyrian vessel, the other
to the barge ; to them Helicanus*

T.S. (*to the Sailor of Mytilene*) Where is Lord Helicanus ?
      he can resolve you.
      O, here he is.
      Sir, there is a barge put off from Mytilene,
      And in it is Lysimachus the governor,
      Who craves to come aboard.   What is your will ?
Hel. That he have his.   Call up some gentlemen.
T.S. Ho, gentlemen ! my lord calls.
            Enter two or three Gentlemen
1.G. Doth your lordship call ?

Hel. Gentlemen, there is some of worth would come
    aboard ; I pray, greet him fairly.   10

> *The Gentlemen and the two Sailors descend,*
> *and go on board the barge*
> *Enter from thence, Lysimachus, and Lords ; with the*
> *Gentlemen and the two Sailors*

T.S. Sir,
    This is the man that can, in aught you would,
    Resolve you.

Lys. Hail, reverend sir ! the gods preserve you !

Hel. And you, sir, to outlive the age I am,
    And die as I would do.

Lys.   You wish me well.
    Being on shore, honouring of Neptune's triumphs,
    Seeing this goodly vessel ride before us,
    I made to it, to know of whence you are.

Hel. First, what is your place ?   20

Lys. I am the governor of this place you lie before.

Hel. Sir,
    Our vessel is of Tyre, in it the king ;
    A man who for this three months hath not spoken
    To any one, nor taken sustenance
    But to prorogue his grief.

Lys. Upon what ground is his distemperature ?

Hel. 'Twould be too tedious to repeat ;

But the main grief springs from the loss
Of a beloved daughter and a wife.   30

Lys. May we not see him ?

Hel. You may ;
But bootless is your sight ; he will not speak
To any.

Lys. Yet let me obtain my wish.

Hel. Behold him. (*Pericles discovered*) This was a goodly
    person,
Till the disaster that, one mortal night,
Drove him to this.

Lys. Sir king, all hail ! the gods preserve you !
Hail, royal sir !   40

Hel. It is in vain ; he will not speak to you.

1.L. Sir,
We have a maid in Mytilene, I durst wager,
Would win some words of him.

Lys.   'Tis well bethought.
She, questionless, with her sweet harmony
And other chosen attractions, would allure,
And make a battery through his deafen'd parts,
Which now are midway stopp'd :
She is all happy as the fairest of all,
And with her fellow maids is now upon   50
The leafy shelter that abuts against

The island's side.   *Whispers a Lord, who goes off*
                                          in the barge of Lysimachus

Hel. Sure, all's effectless ; yet nothing we'll omit
   That bears recovery's name.   But, since your kind-
         ness
   We have stretch'd thus far, let us beseech you
   That for our gold we may provision have,
   Wherein we are not destitute for want,
   But weary for the staleness.

Lys.   O, sir, a courtesy
   Which if we should deny, the most just gods
   For every graff would send a caterpillar,   60
   And so inflict our province.   Yet once more
   Let me entreat to know at large the cause
   Of your king's sorrow.

Hel.   Sit, sir, I will recount it to you.
   But, see, I am prevented.

         Re-enter, from the barge, Lord, with Marina, and
                        a young Lady

Lys.   O, here is
   The lady that I sent for.   Welcome, fair one !—
   Is 't not a goodly presence ?

Hel.   She 's a gallant lady.

Lys. She 's such a one, that, were I well assur'd
   Came of a gentle kind and noble stock,

I 'ld wish no better choice, and think me rarely wed.
Fair one, all goodness that consists in bounty   70
Expect even here, where is a kingly patient:
If that thy prosperous and artificial feat
Can draw him but to answer thee in aught,
Thy sacred physic shall receive such pay
As thy desires can wish.

Mar.   Sir, I will use
My utmost skill in his recovery, provided
That none but I and my companion maid
Be suffer'd to come near him.

Lys.   Come, let us leave her;
And the gods make her prosperous!   *Marina sings*

Lys. Mark'd he your music?

Mar.   No, nor look'd on us.   80

Lys. See, she will speak to him.

Mar. Hail, sir! my lord, lend ear.

Per. Hum, ha!

Mar. I am a maid,
My lord, that ne'er before invited eyes,
But have been gaz'd on like a comet: she speaks,
My lord, that, may be, hath endur'd a grief
Might equal yours, if both were justly weigh'd.
Though wayward fortune did malign my state,
My derivation was from ancestors   90

Who stood equivalent with mighty kings :
But time hath rooted out my parentage,
And to the world and awkward casualties
Bound me in servitude.   (*aside*) I will desist ;
But there is something glows upon my cheek,
And whispers in mine ear ' Go not till he speak.'

Per. My fortunes—parentage—good parentage—
To equal mine !—was it not thus ? what say you ?

Mar. I said, my lord, if you did know my parentage,
You would not do me violence.   100

Per. I do think so.   Pray you, turn your eyes upon me.
You are like something that—What countrywoman ?
Here of these shores ?

Mar.   No, nor of any shores :
Yet I was mortally brought forth, and am
No other than I appear.

Per. I am great with woe, and shall deliver weeping.
My dearest wife was like this maid, and such a one
My daughter might have been : my queen's square
        brows ;
Her stature to an inch ; as wand-like straight,
As silver-voic'd, her eyes as jewel-like,   110
And cas'd as richly, in pace another Juno ;
Who starves the ears she feeds, and makes them
        hungry,

97

      The more she gives them speech.   Where do you live?

Mar. Where I am but a stranger: from the deck
    You may discern the place.

Per.   Where were you bred?
    And how achiev'd you these endowments, which
    You make more rich to owe?

Mar. If I should tell my history, it would seem
    Like lies disdain'd in the reporting.

Per.   Prithee, speak:
    Falseness cannot come from thee, for thou look'st   120
    Modest as Justice, and thou seem'st a palace
    For the crown'd Truth to dwell in: I will believe
        thee,
    And make my senses credit thy relation
    To points that seem impossible, for thou look'st
    Like one I lov'd indeed.   What were thy friends?
    Didst thou not say, when I did push thee back—
    Which was when I perceiv'd thee—that thou cam'st
    From good descending?

Mar.   So indeed I did.

Per. Report thy parentage.   I think thou said'st
    Thou hadst been toss'd from wrong to injury,   130
    And that thou thought'st thy griefs might equal mine,
    If both were open'd.

Mar.   Some such thing

I said, and said no more but what my thoughts
Did warrant me was likely.

Per.   Tell thy story ;
If thine consider'd prove the thousandth part
Of my endurance, thou art a man, and I
Have suffer'd like a girl : yet thou dost look
Like Patience gazing on kings' graves and smiling
Extremity out of act.   What were thy friends ?
How lost thou them ?   Thy name, my most kind
    virgin ?   140
Recount, I do beseech thee : come, sit by me.

Mar. My name is Marina.

Per.   O, I am mock'd,
And thou by some incensed god sent hither
To make the world to laugh at me.

Mar.   Patience, good sir,
Or here I 'll cease.

Per.   Nay, I 'll be patient.
Thou little know'st how thou dost startle me,
To call thyself Marina.

Mar.   The name
Was given me by one that had some power,
My father, and a king.

Per.   How, a king's daughter ?
And call'd Marina ?

Mar.   You said you would believe me ; 150
    But, not to be a troubler of your peace,
    I will end here.

Per.   But are you flesh and blood ?
    Have you a working pulse, and are no fairy ?
    No motion ? Well ; speak on. Where were you
       born ?
    And wherefore call'd Marina ?

Mar.   Call'd Marina
    For I was born at sea.

Per.   At sea ? what mother ?

Mar. My mother was the daughter of a king ;
    Who died the minute I was born,
    As my good nurse Lychorida hath oft
    Deliver'd weeping.

Per.   O, stop there a little !   160
    (aside) This is the rarest dream that e'er dull'd sleep
    Did mock sad fools withal : this cannot be :
    My daughter 's buried.—Well : where were you bred ?
    I 'll hear you more, to the bottom of your story,
    And never interrupt you.

Mar. You scorn : believe me, 'twere best I did give o'er. †

Per. I will believe you by the syllable
    Of what you shall deliver.   Yet, give me leave :
    How came you in these parts ? where were you bred ?

Mar. The king my father did in Tarsus leave me,   170
　　　Till cruel Cleon, with his wicked wife,
　　　Did seek to murder me : and having woo'd
　　　A villain to attempt it, who having drawn to do 't,
　　　A crew of pirates came and rescued me ;
　　　Brought me to Mytilene.   But, good sir, whither
　　　Will you have me ?   Why do you weep ?   It may be,
　　　You think me an impostor : no, good faith ;
　　　I am the daughter to King Pericles,
　　　If good King Pericles be.

Per. Ho, Helicanus !   180

Hel. Calls my lord ?

Per. Thou art a grave and noble counsellor,
　　　Most wise in general : tell me, if thou canst,
　　　What this maid is, or what is like to be,
　　　That thus hath made me weep.

Hel. 　　　　　　　　　　I know not ; but
　　　Here is the regent, sir, of Mytilene
　　　Speaks nobly of her.

Lys. 　　　　　　　She never would tell
　　　Her parentage ; being demanded that,
　　　She would sit still and weep.

Per. O Helicanus, strike me, honour'd sir ;   190
　　　Give me a gash, put me to present pain ;
　　　Lest this great sea of joys rushing upon me

101

O'erbear the shores of my mortality,
And drown me with their sweetness. O, come hither,
Thou that beget'st him that did thee beget:
Thou that wast born at sea, buried at Tarsus,
And found at sea again! O Helicanus,
Down on thy knees; thank the holy gods as loud
As thunder threatens us: this is Marina.
What was thy mother's name? tell me but that,   200
For truth can never be confirm'd enough,
Though doubts did ever sleep.

*Mar.*First, sir, I pray, what is your title?

Per.   I

Am Pericles of Tyre: but tell me now
My drown'd queen's name, as in the rest you said
Thou hast been godlike perfect, the heir of kingdoms,
And another like to Pericles thy father.

*Mar.*Is it no more to be your daughter than
To say my mother's name was Thaisa?
Thaisa was my mother, who did end   210
The minute I began.

Per. Now, blessing on thee! rise; thou art my child.
Give me fresh garments. Mine own, Helicanus:
She is not dead at Tarsus, as she should have been,
By savage Cleon: she shall tell thee all;
When thou shalt kneel, and justify in knowledge

      She is thy very princess.   Who is this?

Hel. Sir, 'tis the governor of Mytilene,

      Who, hearing of your melancholy state,

      Did come to see you.   220

Per. I embrace you.

      Give me my robes.   I am wild in my beholding.

      O heavens bless my girl! But, hark, what music?

      Tell Helicanus, my Marina, tell him

      O'er, point by point, for yet he seems to doubt,

      How sure you are my daughter. But, what music?

Hel. My lord, I hear none.

Per. None!

      The music of the spheres! List, my Marina.

Lys. It is not good to cross him; give him way.   230

Per. Rarest sounds!

      Do you not hear?

Lys.   Music, my lord?

Per.   I hear

      Most heavenly music!

      It nips me unto listening, and thick slumber

      Hangs upon mine eyes: let me rest.   *Sleeps*

Lys. A pillow for his head:

      So, leave him all.   Well, my companion friends,

      If this but answer to my just belief,

      I'll well remember you.   *Exeunt all but Pericles*

Diana appears to Pericles in a vision

Dia. My temple stands in Ephesus : hie thee thither,　240
　　　And do upon mine altar sacrifice.
　　　There, when my maiden priests are met together,
　　　Before the people all,
　　　Reveal how thou at sea didst lose thy wife :
　　　To mourn thy crosses, with thy daughter's, call,
　　　And give them repetition to the life.
　　　Or perform my bidding, or thou liv'st in woe ;
　　　Do it, and happy ; by my silver bow !
　　　Awake, and tell thy dream.　　　　*Disappears*

Per. Celestial Dian, goddess argentine,　　250
　　　I will obey thee.　Helicanus !

　　　Re-enter Helicanus, Lysimachus, and Marina

Hel.　　　　　　　　　　Sir ?

Per. My purpose was for Tarsus, there to strike
　　　The inhospitable Cleon ; but I am
　　　For other service first : toward Ephesus
　　　Turn our blown sails ; eftsoons I 'll tell thee why.
　　　(*to Lys.*) Shall we refresh us, sir, upon your shore,
　　　And give you gold for such provision
　　　As our intents will need ?

Lys. Sir,
　　　With all my heart ; and, when you come ashore,　260
　　　I have another suit.

Per.   You shall prevail,
    Were it to woo my daughter ; for it seems
    You have been noble towards her.
Lys.   Sir, lend me your arm.
Per. Come, my Marina.   *Exeunt*

SCENE II

Enter Gower, before the temple of Diana at Ephesus

Gow. Now our sands are almost run ;
    More a little, and then dumb.
    This, my last boon, give me,
    For such kindness must relieve me,
    That you aptly will suppose
    What pageantry, what feats, what shows,
    What minstrelsy and pretty din,
    The regent made in Mytilene,
    To greet the king.   So he thrived,
    That he is promis'd to be wived   10
    To fair Marina ; but in no wise
    Till he had done his sacrifice,
    As Dian bade : whereto being bound,
    The interim pray you all confound.
    In feather'd briefness sails are fill'd,

And wishes fall out as they 're will'd.
At Ephesus, the temple see,
Our king and all his company.
That he can hither come so soon,
Is by your fancies' thankful doom.   *Exit* 20

SCENE III

The temple of Diana at Ephesus ; Thaisa standing near the
altar, as high priestess ; a number of Virgins on each
side ; Cerimon and other Inhabitants of Ephesus attending

Enter Pericles, with his train ; Lysimachus, Helicanus,
Marina, and a Lady

Per. Hail, Dian ! to perform thy just command,
I hear confess myself the king of Tyre ;
Who, frighted from my country, did wed
At Pentapolis the fair Thaisa.
At sea in childbed died she, but brought forth
A maid-child call'd Marina ; who, O goddess,
Wears yet thy silver livery.   She at Tarsus
Was nurs'd with Cleon, who at fourteen years
He sought to murder, but her better stars
Brought her to Mytilene, 'gainst whose shore   10
Riding, her fortunes brought the maid aboard us,

Where, by her own most clear remembrance, she
Made known herself my daughter.

Tha.   Voice and favour!
You are, you are—O royal Pericles!—   *Faints*

Per. What means the nun? she dies! help, gentlemen!

Cer. Noble sir,
If you have told Diana's altar true,
This is your wife.

Per.   Reverend appearer, no;
I threw her overboard with these very arms.

Cer. Upon this coast, I warrant you.

Per.   'Tis most certain.   20

Cer. Look to the lady.   O, she 's but overjoy'd.
Early in blustering morn this lady was
Thrown upon this shore.   I op'd the coffin,
Found there rich jewels, recover'd her, and plac'd her
Here in Diana's temple.

Per.   May we see them?

Cer. Great sir, they shall be brought you to my house,
Whither I invite you.   Look, Thaisa is
Recovered.

Tha. O, let me look!
If he be none of mine, my sanctity   30
Will to my sense bend no licentious ear,
But curb it, spite of seeing.   O, my lord,

Are you not Pericles?   Like him you spake,
Like him you are: did you not name a tempest,
A birth, and death?

Per.   The voice of dead Thaisa!

Tha. That Thaisa am I, supposed dead
And drown'd.

Per. Immortal Dian!

Tha.   Now I know you better.
When we with tears parted Pentapolis,
The king my father gave you such a ring.   40

Shows a ring

Per. This, this: no more, you gods! your present kindness
Makes my past miseries sports: you shall do well,
That on the touching of her lips I may
Melt, and no more be seen.   O, come, be buried
A second time within these arms.

Mar.   My heart
Leaps to be gone into my mother's bosom.

Kneels to Thaisa

Per. Look, who kneels here!   Flesh of thy flesh, Thaisa;
Thy burden at the sea, and call'd Marina
For she was yielded there.

Tha.   Blest, and mine own!

Hel. Hail, madam, and my queen!

Tha.   I know you not.   50

Per. You have heard me say, when I did fly from Tyre,
    I left behind an ancient substitute :
    Can you remember what I call'd the man ?
    I have named him oft.

Tha.   'Twas Helicanus then.

Per. Still confirmation :
    Embrace him, dear Thaisa ; this is he.
    Now do I long to hear how you were found ;
    How possibly preserv'd ; and who to thank,
    Besides the gods, for this great miracle.

Tha. Lord Cerimon, my lord ; this man,   60
    Through whom the gods have shown their power :
        that can
    From first to last resolve you.

Per.   Reverend sir,
    The gods can have no mortal officer
    More like a god than you.   Will you deliver
    How this dead queen re-lives ?

Cer.   I will, my lord.
    Beseech you, first go with me to my house,
    Where shall be shown you all was found with her ;
    How she came plac'd here in the temple ;
    No needful thing omitted.

Per. Pure Dian, I bless thee for thy vision, and   70
    Will offer night-oblations to thee.   Thaisa,

This prince, the fair-betrothed of your daughter,
Shall marry her at Pentapolis.   And now,
This ornament
Makes me look dismal will I clip to form ;
And what this fourteen years no razor touch'd,
To grace thy marriage-day, I'll beautify.

Tha. Lord Cerimon hath letters of good credit, sir,
My father's dead.

Per. Heavens make a star of him !   Yet there, my queen,   80
We'll celebrate their nuptials, and ourselves
Will in that kingdom spend our following days :
Our son and daughter shall in Tyrus reign.
Lord Cerimon, we do our longing stay
To hear the rest untold : sir, lead the way.   *Exeunt*

Enter Gower

Gow. In Antiochus and his daughter you have heard
Of monstrous lust the due and just reward :
In Pericles, his queen and daughter, seen,
Although assail'd with fortune fierce and keen,
Virtue preserved from fell destruction's blast,   90
Led on by heaven and crown'd with joy at last :
In Helicanus may you well descry
A figure of truth, of faith, of loyalty :
In reverend Cerimon there well appears
The worth that learned charity aye wears :

For wicked Cleon and his wife, when fame
Had spread their cursed deed, the honour'd name
Of Pericles, to rage the city turn,
That him and his they in his palace burn;
The gods for murder seemed so content   100
To punish, although not done, but meant.
So, on your patience evermore attending,
New joy wait on you!   Here our play has ending.

Exit

Notes

I have confined the Notes almost entirely to the last three acts. (It is, by the way, noteworthy that the text is much more corrupt in the first two acts than in the last three.) Exactly what unmetrical nonsense Wilkins (if it was Wilkins) talked, or is made to talk by the compositor of Q, or what steps we take to allow him to talk approximate metre and sense, seem to me of trivial importance. I have therefore, in the first two acts, allowed some apparent corruptions to stand, admitted to the text accepted emendations for others without comment, and even in three places (as I have been cautious not to do elsewhere in this edition) inserted without comment readings of my own.

I. i. 27. *Hesperides*; one of the labours of Hercules was to bring back the golden apples of the ' daughters of the sunset,' which were guarded by a dragon. In l. 29 *affright* is unsatisfactory; one wants a word meaning ' stand close to,' and *affront* has been suggested.

II. i. 53-56. Something has evidently gone very wrong here, since there is no possible point in the fisherman's rejoinder as the text stands. Pericles must have said something about a day. Deighton suggests that before *Peace be at your labour* Pericles said *Hoyday!* which seems to start the interchange on the right lines. But I think he misses the point of what follows, by taking *fits* to mean ' is to your liking '; the fisherman means, I think, ' If the day is one that fits the poor bedraggled creature you are, away with it from the calendar and no one will miss it '; and we can emend *search* accordingly; Steevens read *scratch it*.

II. i. 73. *throng'd up*; the Arden editor takes the bull by the

113

horns and says that this means 'shrivelled' or 'clemmed.' I feel
no doubt that this is right and would add 'shrammed' to the
meanings; but it is fair to add that the N.E.D. gives small support
to any meaning more particular and vivid than 'oppressed.'

II. i. 125. *protect thee from*; Q reads *protect thee Fame*; and I
should be inclined to read *The which the gods protect!—the same
defend thee.*

II. i. 130. *my father gave*; so Q; usually emended *to my father's
gift.* But one of the marks of the diction of this play is the large
number of harsh omissions of the relative.

III. i. 35. *portage quit*; a reference to the full entry in N.E.D.
will make this phrase clear. One embarking on a 'merchant-
adventure' was allowed to put on board goods, the profit on
which would be in lieu of wages or of part of his wages. Here
then 'what you have lost is more than can be counterbalanced by
any goods for traffic that you can possibly have on board.'

III. i. 43. *bolins*; a form of 'bowlines,' but that in itself is not
very helpful, since to us a 'bowline' is rather a knot than a sheet.
They were apparently ropes attached to the weather side of a square
sail to aid in trimming it so that the ship would sail as near the
wind as might be.

III. ii. 41. *pleasure*; so Q; almost universally emended to *treasure*
surely a very commonplace reading and less Shakespearean than the
text.

III. ii. 97. *nature awakes;* . . .; this is the ordinary reading, but
I am not sure that Q's reading, *nature awakes a warmth breath*, does
not rather point to *nature awakes a warm breath.*

III. iii. 6. *Your shafts* . . .; Q reads *shakes, hant*, and *wondringly* for
shafts, hurt, and *wanderingly.* I give the ordinary emendation; but
would somewhat prefer Schmidt's *woundingly.*

III. iii. 36. *mask'd*; if this is sound it must mean, I suppose, Neptune who is for the moment masking all his potentialities for storm and fury. Many emendations have been suggested.

III. iv. 6. *eaning*; so F. Q reads *learning*, for which *bearing* would be graphically rather easier.

IV. prol. 28. *rich and constant pen Vail*; if this means anything at all it must mean that she worshipped Dian by writing poetry to her. But though *vail* can no doubt mean ' worship,' it is a very curious word to use of that kind of worship.

IV. i. 1-7. This passage is usually given as verse, though not by either Q or F. And it makes such indifferent verse that I prefer to leave it, not least because it seems more fitting that the verse should not begin till Marina's entrance.

IV. i. 5. *inflaming love i' thy bosom*; this is Knight's reading, usually adopted. Q reads *in flaming thy loue bosome*, and F the same, but joining the first two words to *inflaming*. I am not clear that any of the emendations helps matters much. The sense is clear, that neither conscience nor pity should be allowed to stand in his way.

IV. i. 10. *mistress*; I leave the QF reading, unsatisfactory though it is, since the facile emendation to *nurse's* seems too easy to be true.

IV. i. 62. ' *Ha!*' *says one*, ' *wilt out?*'; one editor suggests perhaps "will you not cease," apostrophising the storm '; and another wants to emend to *wilt thou?* commenting that the sailor is perhaps addressing the shroud which the wind blows out. But why all this complication? The remark is surely just a rather brutally humorous one to the man who has been washed off; ' Must you really be going? '

IV. i. 79. *I trod upon . . .*; I do not think that the emendation of *Nor* for *I* quite meets the case, since *against my will* and *But I wept for it* are really saying the same thing. I would much prefer to transpose ll. 78 and 79 and read:

> *I trod upon a worm against my will,*
> *I never kill'd a mouse, nor hurt a fly,*
> *But I wept for it.*

IV. iii. 46. *harpy*; the mythical creature, a winged fury, that 'snatched' (hence the name) away things, especially banquets before the eyes of the banqueters. Cf. *The Tempest*.

IV. vi. 37. *number*; this, the reading of Q, has been justified, with the meaning 'the profession of modesty gives an air of decency to a bawd, just as it gains for a number of women the credit of being chaste.' That no doubt makes sense, but I cannot believe that any Elizabethan ever wrote so colourless and ill-balanced a sentence. The 'run' surely is 'to be modest dignifies the renown of a bawd, as to be chaste gives a good report to a ——. To fill the gap there have been suggestions as diverse as *pander, lecher, wanton,* and *maiden*.

V. prol. 16. *city's hiv'd*; Steevens' emendation of Q's *city striv'd*.

V. prol. 23. *action*; this phrase seems to be usually taken to mean 'where what is done in action shall be discovered (*i.e.* revealed to you) and more would be if we could do it.' But *action* in that interpretation seems oddly redundant, and I feel that the sense is rather 'where what is done shall be represented in our acting of it, and we would make the representation more complete if we could'; i.e. *in action* goes with *shall be discovered*, not with *done*.

V. i. 166. *You scorn*; so Q. But this will hardly do, since there has been no sign of scorn. Malone's *You'll scarce believe* is tempting

Glossary

MANY words and phrases in Shakespeare require glossing, not because they are in themselves unfamiliar, but for the opposite reason, that Shakespeare uses in their Elizabethan and unfamiliar sense a large number of words which seem so familiar that there is no incentive to look for them in the glossary. It is hoped that a glossary arranged as below will make it easy to see at a glance what words and phrases in any particular scene require elucidation. A number of phrases are glossed by what seems to be, in their context, the modern equivalent rather than by lexicographical glosses on the words which compose them.

Act First

BEFORE THE PALACE OF ANTIOCH

line
21 FERE, mate
24 HIS, its

line
32 FRAME, *sc.* their course
40 YON GRIM LOOKS, *i.e.* the be-headed heads (*cf.* I. i. 36)

SCENE I

8 LUCINA, goddess of childbirth
40 ON DEATH'S NET, into death's snare
93 BRAID, touch
101 COPP'D, round-topped

101 THRONG'D, overwhelmed
110 GLOZE, quibble
152 PARTAKES, shares out
165 LEVEL, aim

SCENE II

25 OSTENT, display
38 DO ABUSE, are disloyal to
48 LADING, cargo

86 DOUBT, suspect
109 DIRECT, delegate

SCENE IV

line		line	
9	TOPP'D, pollarded	43	CURIOUS, superfine
26	JETTED, strutted	61	PORTLY SAIL, impressive fleet
	ADORN'D, *sc.* themselves	83	CONSIST, agree
27	GLASS, mirror	92	HAPPILY, haply
42	NOUSLE, nurse		

Act Second

ENTER GOWER

4 AWFUL, awe-inspiring

DUMB SHOW

40 LONGS THE TEXT, belongs to the
    action of the play

SCENE I

17	WITH A WANION, with a vengeance	126	KEPT, lodged
73	THRONG'D, oppressed	145	CONDOLEMENT, solatium
83	FLAP-JACKS, pancakes		VAILS, 'tips'
123	BRACE, (?) suit of armour	150	RAPTURE, snatching
		156	PAIR OF BASES, a kind of kilt

SCENE II

1	TRIUMPH, display	30	ME POMPAE PROVEXIT APEX, the summit of honour has led me on
4	RETURN, reply to		
21	LUX TUA VITA MIHI, thy light my life	33	QUOD ME ALIT, ME EXTINGUIT, what feeds me quenches me
27-28	PIU POR DULZURA QUE POR FUERZA, more by sweetness than by force	38	SIC SPECTANDA FIDES, thus must faith be tried
		51	WHIPSTOCK, whipping-post

SCENE III

line

29 RESIST ME, HE BUT THOUGHT
UPON, mislike me, as soon as
I think of him

42 VAIL, bow

line

70 IMPUDENCE, shamelessness

95 ADDRESS'D, arrayed

105 MEASURES, dancing-steps

SCENE IV

3 MINDING, intending

35 STRONGEST, most probable

35 CENSURE, opinion

44 TAKE I, if I take

SCENE V

20 MINDING, caring

Act Third

ENTER GOWER

4 POMPOUS, splendid

13 ECHE, eke out

DUMB SHOW

1 DERN, drear
PERCH, measure of land (*prop.*
5½ yards)

3 COIGNS, corners

21 STEAD, forward

55 NILL, will not

SCENE I

16 CONCEIT, intelligence

61 FOR, instead of

62 AYE-REMAINING LAMPS, the lamp
in the vault, always burning

PERICLES

SCENE II

Act Fourth

ENTER GOWER

SCENE I

SCENE II

SCENE III

SCENE IV

line

2 HAVE AND WISH BUT FOR 'T, have by wishing

10 THWARTING, traversing

line

18 PILOT, *adj.*

19 STEERAGE, steering

41 THETIS, sea-goddess

SCENE VI

17 LOWN, loon, yokel

60 MANAGE, control (from horse-training, manège)

90 PUT UPON YOU, invested with it

105 BE YOU THOUGHTEN, believe

120 COPE, vault of sky

161 COISTREL, oaf

Act Fifth

ENTER GOWER

8 INKLE, yarn

SCENE I

26 PROROGUE, keep alive

60 GRAFF, scion

72 ARTIFICIAL FEAT, exercise of art

93 AWKWARD CASUALTIES, sinister chances

117 TO OWE, in owning

250 ARGENTINE, silver

255 EFTSOONS, soon

SCENE II

279 FEATHER'D BRIEFNESS, winged speed

SCENE III

18 APPEARER, one who suddenly appears

49 YIELDED, born